Reaching People

from the Pulpit

Reaching People from the Pulpit

A GUIDE TO
EFFECTIVE SERMON DELIVERY

by

DWIGHT E. STEVENSON

and

CHARLES F. DIEHL

BAKER BOOK HOUSE
Grand Rapids, Michigan

Library of Congress catalog card number: 58-7104

ISBN: 0-8010-8133-5

First printing, May 1978
Second printing, March 1980
Third printing, October 1982
Fourth printing, June 1985

PHOTOLITHOPRINTED BY CUSHING - MALLOY, INC.
ANN ARBOR, MICHIGAN, UNITED STATES OF AMERICA

Contents

Illustrations

Foreword

There are scores of books on sermon preparation but exceedingly few on sermon delivery. This is a book devoted exclusively to the problems of delivery.

It has been written both for seminary students and for settled ministers. The book offers itself most obviously to classes, workshops, and clinics in preaching which may be formed in or out of seminary. But it can also serve as a self-help manual which an individual minister may use without being in a class.

In scope, the book covers all the topics essential to effective oral communication. As customarily summarized, these are: respiration, phonation, articulation, resonation, and integration. In other words, the book covers all the basic skills of oral speech from breathing to the mastery of notes at the creative moment of delivery. The key to the method of the book is analytical listening. "The door to the tongue is the ear." From this base line, the reader is shown what to listen for and how to listen in rating the speeches and sermons of other men. And he is led gradually, through the use of tape recording, to listen to and analyze his own speaking.

As each man discovers his own areas of need, he is pointed directly to remedial exercises in Appendix C and is given a method of working by which he may incorporate his gains first into conversation and into public reading, then finally into the ultimate act of sermon delivery.

There are three rating scales: (1) for the voice variables, (2) for the use of the body, and (3) for the emotional factors commonly known as *melism* and *pathos*; these are basic tools which the reader will want to mimeograph in quantity for his own use. They will be found in Appendix A. The last two chapters of the book give step-by-step guidance for the conduct of a preaching workshop and for an individual program of self-help.

The authors work on adjoining campuses, one at a state university as head of the speech center, the other at a theological seminary as a teacher of homiletics. Recently they have collaborated in several speech clinics for theological students. This association led rather naturally to the present book.

They are indebted to many people for direct and indirect help in producing this volume. Not least among these are their own students, who were enthusiastic partners in giving the methods of the book the pragmatic test.

Some of the material first published in *The Pastor Magazine* as a series under the title, "We Do Preach Ourselves," has been drawn upon and cast into a different form. The same is true of an article, "Misreading the Bible in Public," in *The Pulpit Digest*, and another article, "What Happened to the Sermon?" in *The Christian Evangelist*. The writers are grateful to the editors of these journals for permission to draw upon these articles and to reshape the treatment to the present purpose. Biblical quotations are from the Revised Standard Version and are used by permission of the Division of Christian Education of the National Council of Churches of Christ in the U.S.A.

Quite a number of people were involved during the actual writing of this book. They read the manuscript chapter by chapter as it was being produced and offered numerous criticisms which resulted in several improvements. Among those who thus helped special thanks go to: Richard C. White (who both read the manuscript and drew the sketches), Barbara Wilson, Marian Coates, Rose Shrimpton, William Clayton Bower, and DeLoris Stevenson.

Dwight E. Stevenson

Lexington, Kentucky   Charles F. Diehl

Reaching People

from the Pulpit

1.   *The Sound of Your Sermon*

One of the most important things a minister does week by week is to deliver his sermons to his people. It is then and only then that the fire in his soul is or is not communicated. It is then and only then that the long years of college and seminary education find their target or miss it altogether. It is then that the hours in the study preparing the sermon are ratified or nullified.

The delivery of a sermon is a profoundly searching experience for the preacher himself. It has to do with a great deal more than a few techniques. It probes a man, mind and soul. The spoken sermon is the point at which the whole of a man's life and training comes most vividly into focus. What a man has to give by way of intellect, training, human understanding, moral integrity, and spiritual awareness is centered in the pulpit at the creative moment of delivery. By the same token, what a man needs in his growth toward Christian maturity is also glaringly apparent at this same point.

Thus, the spoken sermon is the index of the man who delivers it. If this were all, there would be reason enough why a minister should always regard his own sermon delivery as unfinished business, to be studied and improved throughout his ministry. But there is more. The spoken sermon is the focal point of the Gospel in contemporary life. It is at the pulpit that the timeless Word is made timely or stagnates in an antiquarian morass. It is at the pulpit that its claims are made relevant or evaporate into ir-relevance. It is at the pulpit that eternity speaks to mortality, or else it is there that mediocrity and this-worldliness wash in as a sea inundating all dikes. If the Gospel is alive in this generation it must be alive in the spoken sermon. Not merely in the study, or on the paper of a manuscript, but in the creative moment of oral delivery.

There is still more. The spoken sermon is communicated; that is why it is spoken. It both creates and depends upon an interper-sonal world. That is to say that the state of health in the Christian community is indicated by the pulpit. Is the sermon a solo per-formance by a skilled ecclesiastical actor? Is the congregation re-duced to an audience? Then we have no sermon, for we have no Christian community. A man preaching a sermon, therefore, has something more to do than speak his own mind; he has to be the voice of the Church as community. The oral sermon, then, "is the ideal Church addressing the actual, the upper Church the lower, the Church of the ages appealing to the Church of the hour, the Church universal to the Church on the spot."[1]

Thus from within its own dynamic, the spoken sermon becomes a crucial concern for the minister and the Church. To these urgent reasons for paying heed to how we speak, the world itself now adds another: the challenge of the mass communication media. In this voice-conscious age—radio and TV have made us that way—it seems inevitable that undisciplined ministerial voices will ulti-mately grate on people's ears. The ministers of the new generation will simply have to live up to a higher standard.

Excellence in the preparation of sermons does not necessarily carry with it excellence in delivery, nor is excellence in delivery always a mark of good preparation and sound substance. We have all seen this in other speakers. On occasion we have sat with other listeners swayed by a man's eloquence and ready to say, like the enraptured audience before Herod, "It is the voice of a god!" Afterward we have left the meeting, escaped from the spell of that

[1] P. T. Forsyth, *Positive Preaching and the Modern Mind* (Independent Press, 1907), p. 64.

speaker's voice, and asked ourselves, "What did he say now really?" In all honesty we could only answer. "He said hardly anything; it was all in the way he said it. As for the worth of his ideas, it might as well have been the braying of an ass—and perhaps it was."

On the other hand, we have more than once listened to an excellent speech or marvelous sermon so poorly delivered that not more than 5 percent of the hearers had any idea of the importance of what they were hearing. In the realm of ideas the lightning flashed, the thunder roared, the heavens opened as the voice of God rolled forth, but not more than a man here and there throughout the congregation had any awareness of what was going on. The rest of the people just sat and endured it. They heard no voice of God; they heard a man mumbling, and—mentally at least—they fell asleep. They could only wait in patience for the final hymn and the benediction to bring about their deliverance.

We all know these things happen—to other preachers. We like to think that we are exceptions—that our delivery is really pretty good. Indications are that such subjective judgments are seldom reliable.

For the average student in training in a seminary there is still time. As a part of his regular curriculum he can in most cases take full advantage of whatever courses are offered in speech and homiletics. He may in some instances enroll for additional training in special classes or workshops for improving delivery. The entire seminary with all its staff and facilities is still available to the interested student. But what is the situation of the average practicing minister in this matter? He is really alone. If he wants to know how well he is "getting across" he can only consult his own feelings, which are usually highly subjective and unreliable; or ask his wife's opinion, which is prone to be almost as biased as his. He knows that the members of the congregation talk about his preaching. They must! But word of what they are saying seldom reaches him. A few flatter him to his face. It is easy to be misled by such flattery. Six people indulging in it on a Sunday after church can blind him to the fact that three hundred people were perfunctory or diffident in their responses. A few—fewer still—speak out bluntly in criticism now and then; they seldom speak to help him.

For the seminary student there is still time. The average minister may feel that he is largely without resources. Nevertheless, either man can begin where he is—in the parish or in the seminary—and he can work out with the aid of this book a program to evaluate his delivery and improve it if necessary.

We shall say more about procedure shortly. First, let us consider certain norms or standards for effective delivery.

WHEN IS DELIVERY DEFECTIVE?

There is general agreement among speech specialists that one's speech needs corrective treatment under one or more of the following conditions:

a. If it calls attention to itself.

b. If it interferes with effective communication.

c. If it creates self-consciousness and causes anxiety.

A man trying to use the above criteria in determining his own needs will soon find that he cannot be certain about any one of them except the third. If he is self-conscious about his speech he will know it, and no other person will know it half so well. On the other hand, he may have decided years ago that his speech is quite adequate or even very effective; yet many people may think he has an unpleasant voice; they may even talk about this among themselves, but never whisper a word of their criticism to him. Furthermore, there is always the possibility that his communication could be a great deal more effective than it is, but that he may be completely unaware of his own capacities. He is left with an unhappy conclusion: His own judgment is unreliable. He needs more criteria. We therefore submit to him the following questions:

1. Do you ever have trouble with your throat after speaking? Are you hoarse at such times? Does your throat feel strained or tired?

2. What is the quality of the attention given you by your congregation? Are people restless? Do they listen avidly or stolidly? Are they eager or merely tolerant?

3. Do you know your own speech machine—as a good mechanic

knows his automobile—or are you merely content to drive it and hope that everything is in good working order?

4. Do you actually know the many different elements that enter into effective vocal expression? Are you making the best use of them?

5. Have you ever had your speaking voice analyzed?

6. Did you ever think about the emotional message which people get from you? What do you feel about yourself, about people, about preaching itself?

7. What do you do with your body in speaking? Do you merely take it along because you can't get away from it or is it really in the speaking, a vital part of it?

8. Have you ever really settled that difficult question about the use of notes or manuscript?

There are other questions that we might ask, but these are sufficient to indicate the drift of our thinking. A quick survey of the questions just asked will supply us with three additional criteria, more meaningful perhaps than the three with which we started. They are:

    a. Speaking ease.

    b. Listener response.

    c. Knowledge and skillful use of all voice factors.

Let us look at each of these briefly in turn.

SPEAKING EASE

We do not mean to say that speaking is not work. On the contrary, it has been estimated that a one-hour speech is the equivalent of six hours of manual labor. To speak loudly the single sound of *b* (as in *ball*) requires the use of at least ninety-five different muscles in our bodies. Effective speaking requires a considerable expenditure of energy and will frequently leave the speaker tired. But there is a vast difference between fatigue and frustration. It is the absence of frustration that we are talking about.

When he is speaking as he was meant to speak a person will stand comfortably, breathe easily, and produce words without excessive tension in any part of the speech musculature. His tones will be free and clear, and when he is finished his voice will not be hoarse or his throat sore. Moreover, he will be master of his situation. He will not be lost in his notes or his ideas, oblivious to the people before him. He will be vividly aware of his listeners and he will take pleasure in sharing his thoughts with them.

Speaking ease will make itself known in the aftermath. Some men suffer a terrific emotional recoil from their preaching. Sometimes they walk on clouds, exalted to the skies by an exhilaration, a kind of intoxication of pleasure and self-approval that lasts for days. But there are other times. Then they feel glum and depressed; the following day is blue Monday, and even Tuesday and Wednesday are a little murky. We have known ministers who suffered migraine headaches nearly every Monday. In either of these cases —exhilaration or depression—there is too much recoil. The speaking has been too difficult. The aftermath should be pleasant and satisfying, but it should leave a man free to accept himself and to go about his work.

LISTENER RESPONSE

There are degrees of listening and ways of listening. If you have sat on the platform at a convention or other public gathering you may have noticed how differently the same audience responds to various speakers. To one speaker the people give close, thoughtful attention. Their eyes seem riveted to him, but they are unsmiling. To another speaker the people give even closer attention; they lean forward eagerly as if to catch his words lest some of them fall to the floor or bounce off the wall. They smile, or laugh aloud, they frown or look thoughtful; their response keeps changing with the changing content of the speaker's thought. They are with him. They are lost in his message and time flows past them unnoticed. To a third speaker the very same people turn a blank stare, which gradually becomes a wandering gaze. Fidgeting sets in. A number of them consult their watches. They all put on masks and sit poker-faced, unthoughtful and unsmiling. At best they are enduring something; at worst they are sorry they came and wish they could think of some graceful way of getting out without being noticed. Time drags and the speaker bores them to distraction.

One way of testing your own speaking is to check it against the response of your listeners. With what degree of attention and pleasure are they listening?

But speaker-audience response is a two-way street. Some men are not aware of how their hearers are reacting. They simply do not see individuals sitting before them; they see a crowd as a blurred mass. They are so wrapped up in their own thoughts that they get no signals from the congregation. They are carrying on a soliloquy when they ought to be engaging in dialogue. They are declaiming at people when they ought to be carrying on a conversation with them. And as for the electric spark which in vital delivery leaps between pulpit and pew, they never experience it.

KNOWLEDGE AND SKILLFUL USE OF ALL VOICE FACTORS

We are educated to see the printed page rather than to hear the spoken word. This is vividly demonstrated by the contrast between missionary husbands and wives in learning a new language. The husbands, conditioned by twenty or more years of classrooms and libraries, are generally slower to speak a new tongue than their wives, and both wives and husbands are usually slower than their preschool children. They simply do not hear it as accurately. When it comes to foreign-language conversation, children spurt ahead of parents, and wives spurt ahead of husbands. The education of the printed page teaches men to see but not to listen.

The fact is that we are rarely aware of the unprinted elements of oral expression. As we will soon see in the Voice Rating Sheet, there are, in one way of counting, not less than sixteen elements of oral speech that can never be communicated to the eye; they must be heard by the ear. The appropriate use of all of them is necessary for effective speaking. Facing this impressive fact, a minister should ask himself three questions:

"Do I know what these sixteen elements of speech are?"

"Do I know how well I am using each of them?"

"At what points do I need to improve?"

In considering the skillful use of voice, it cannot be assumed that a minister has learned or is learning all he ought to know in college or seminary and that he can safely coast on it ever after. Concert pianists never give up practicing. Nor do singers. A trained voice will depend in part, at least, upon drill which is carried out across the years. Even supposing that a man did master it all at once, we have to ask, "What has he done about it since? Is he letting it waste away?" There are people who once played the piano professionally who cannot now get through a hymn without hitting a fistful of wrong notes. Skills are perpetuated through discipline; they are kept alive and alert through practice. Ministers have seldom thought of their sermon delivery in this light, but why not?

So much for a few reasons why practicing ministers or ministers-in-training might want to check up on their own speaking.

WHAT YOU NEED TO GET STARTED

Rating Sheet

A Voice Rating Sheet (see Appendix A, p. 133) is an instrument for analyzing speeches—your own and those of other speakers. This sheet will be discussed in detail in Chapter 3, but for the present the general meaning of the instrument will be immediately apparent. As you give the sheet a short preliminary study, you will notice that there is no provision whatever for the content or organization of speeches, for psychology of approach, for types of speeches, for methods of gathering and filing material, and for getting started with an idea. These are all extremely important factors, but they will not be considered in this book. Here the focus will be upon delivery.

In a live sermon, of course, preparation, content, and delivery go together and cannot be separated. But after a sermon has been delivered and recorded, it is possible to go back to it and listen to certain aspects of it in abstraction, one after the other. That is, we could listen merely to the illustrations and how they are blended into the thought of the sermon, or to the grammar, or to the choice of words, or to the outline; there are any number of factors which could be isolated for particular study. It is through such isolation and focusing that we come to understand the communication process and to set up disciplines for improving it. In this present study you will learn to exclude from attention *what* you have said and concentrate upon *how* you have said it.

This will mean, for example, that inflection and articulation of words will be studied, but not the choice of the words themselves; that attention will be given to phrasing and to pauses but not to grammar. It is obvious, of course, that at first no one can listen to all factors of delivery at the same time. How much more obvious it is, then, that one will fail miserably if he tries to listen to content, organization, grammar, diction, illustration, and delivery all at the same time! Self-analysis often fails not because we are incapable but because we set ourselves an impossible task by attempting too much at one time. In this analysis of sermon delivery the scope has been limited. One factor at a time—voice quality, for example—is isolated for study; then come one or two others, and so on until all factors have been examined.

A *Tape Recorder*

It is needless to point out that such isolation of factors during the actual delivery of a sermon would be disastrous. A man who begins wondering, "How is my inflection? Do I have a pitch pattern?" and asking other critical questions while he is delivering his sermon will end up in frustration. Creative delivery and criticism of that delivery cannot be mixed. They must be separated and applied at different times. The tape recorder makes this possible. With this machine a sermon can be delivered as a living unity of preparation, content, and delivery—as it is meant to be, with critical faculties at rest and creative faculties alert. Then, at a later time, that sermon can be listened to analytically and its parts evaluated.

However, even with a tape recorder it will be necessary to learn how to listen to yourself. As we shall indicate in the next chapter, this is a great deal more difficult than it seems. In the meantime, while you educate your ear and learn what to listen for, there is immediate help of a very practical and highly reliable sort:

Someone to Help You Listen to Yourself

The prime reason for getting someone to help you listen to yourself, even from a faithful recording, is that it is difficult to arrive at an objective judgment alone. A minister can, of course, be helped, and helped greatly, by recording and analyzing his sermons by himself. In some instances this may be necessary. For maximum benefit, however, an objective listener is recommended.

There are a great variety of circumstances in which listening help is possible. It may be in a seminary class in practice preaching. It may come in a summer workshop or preaching clinic. Many such are springing up now, not only under seminary auspices, but in ministers' retreats and institutes with or without official sponsorship from ecclesiastical bodies. The ministers of a local community can create their own preaching workshop. Or an individual minister, unable to participate in any of these group arrangements, may rely upon the help of a single discerning friend.

The main thing to see is that each man in his own situation can, with a little effort, find out just how well he is preaching. Then he can go on with the resources at hand to raise his own level of performance. He can do this at any stage of his career: while he is still in seminary, or in the first crucial years of his active ministry when he is finding his way and forming his habits, or in the mature years when he may have settled down, not too comfortably, into a pattern. There are probably few ministers who feel that they are preaching as well as they can or as well as they would like.

2. *Getting Ready to Hear Yourself*

What you will do with your tongue depends largely on what you are doing with your ears. Most of us learned to talk in our infant years by listening to the speech of those around us. A deaf-mute, on the other hand, is usually mute only because he is deaf. He could speak normally if he could hear. Of course, many deaf people do learn to talk, chiefly through kinesthesia or other special methods. And when a deaf person learns to talk it is unquestionably a superlative achievement. Nevertheless, no deaf person can ever learn to talk with the flexibility of pitch, ease, and spontaneity of a hearing person. For the overwhelming majority, the door to the tongue is the ear.

But now we come to a sobering fact. Most of us, equipped with perfectly normal ears, behave as though we were just a little deaf. We are like the husband in this scrap of evening conversation:

WIFE: ". . . and I told Alice to call you about it tomorrow."
HUSBAND (*engrossed in the evening paper*): "Um."
WIFE: "George, are you listening to me?"
HUSBAND (*reluctantly putting down the paper*): "Well, I heard you, but I wasn't listening."

That is the way it is with most of us. Many hear, but few listen. Indeed, it might be helpful to devise tests for evaluating our listening ability. This special ability might be called the L.Q. (listening quotient), and if it were adequately popularized, knowing one's L.Q. might become as fashionable as knowing one's I.Q. In any event, we all might become more interested in listening. The average person in ordinary conversation unfortunately gets by quite easily even with a very low L.Q. Listening only halfheartedly to others, he expects and generally receives no better treatment from them. At least he hears what *he* has to say, or so he supposes, and to his ears it probably sounds almost eloquent.

This same individual, on the other hand, will probably fall short as a public speaker. To begin with, his frame of reference is almost entirely limited to the way he thinks he sounds. Never having really listened to anyone else, or to himself, for that matter, he has acquired no standards of excellence and has nothing with which to compare his own efforts. And so he may run words together, swallow vowels, drop consonants, sing to a pitch pattern, or chant in a monotone but secretly decide that his performance is quite admirable. He simply does not hear how he sounds.

LISTENING TO OTHERS

So we arrive at an important principle: *If you want to improve your own speech, learn how to listen to other speakers.*

Shortly we shall want you to embark on a more systematic program of listening, but for the present we suggest that you undertake a few preliminary explorations.

In the next day or so, wherever you go—into stores, offices, waiting rooms, classrooms, or on the street—you will hear talking in which you are not directly involved. You may even hear a few speeches on radio or television. Listen; and as you listen, put to each voice a kind of silent questionnaire:

"What about the sound of this voice? Is it harsh, or nasal, or does it seem pleasant? If it is pleasant, why?

"Are words articulated clearly and distinctly? Can I hear and understand easily?

"What is the speaker feeling at the moment? Is he happy or glum; rested or tired; friendly or defensive; high-strung or relaxed?"

You will not be able to answer all the questions at once. Take them one at a time, devoting attention to each in turn. You may be surprised at your progress. Almost certainly your listening will sharpen.

While you are engaged in these preliminary exercises in listening to others you will also want to start thinking about listening to yourself.

LISTENING TO YOURSELF

Just as self-knowledge is believed to be the most difficult of all kinds of knowledge, so listening to oneself is the most difficult of all listening. And if our ears are dull when hearing other people, they are doubly dull when hearing ourselves. There are several reasons for this, some physical, some mental.

Consider some of the physical reasons. When listening to someone else, we hear his voice as vibrations in the air striking our eardrums. But when listening to ourselves, we hear not only these air vibrations but also our own internal vibrations of the larynx, head bones, and sinuses. These internal vibrations account for the fact that we sound deeper, richer, more resonant to ourselves than we do to others. We might refer to the air vibrations as the *external voice* and to the internal vibration as the *internal voice*. Obviously, a speaker hears both voices at the same time, one strengthening the other; but the people listening hear the external voice only.

To hear your own internal voice try this experiment: Stop your ears with the tips of your fingers, or with a wad of cotton. Then speak a few words aloud. The voice you hear under these circumstances is your internal voice. Nobody but you can hear it.

So much for the physical reasons why we do not hear ourselves as others hear us. There are also mental and emotional reasons. The mental reason is simple. When we talk, we are busy thinking —so busy with what we are saying, in fact, that we cannot possibly pay much attention to how we are talking. This is as it should be. If we tried to change it, we would end in confusion.

To the physical and mental factors in our hearing of ourselves the emotional ones are added; our confusion is compounded. If a person has a normal amount of ego, the voice he hears is pleasantly mixed in his mind with the voice he wants to hear. It is rather like looking at oneself in a mirror; the face one sees is one part vision, one part memory, and one part hope.

Let us recapitulate. We cannot hear ourselves as we sound to others for three reasons: (1) Each of us has an internal voice which he alone can hear. (2) We are so busy thinking when we talk that we have no time to listen, even if we could hear ourselves properly. (3) Our emotions enter and each of us hears a pleasant voice, not because it is really there, but because we want it to be pleasant. Listening to oneself is very difficult.

Fortunately, we are living in the age of electronics and we have the priceless boon of tape recording. We do not mean to say that anyone entirely enjoys listening to his own recordings. We have found, on the contrary, that for some the first sessions with a tape recorder are painful. It is normal to say, "I don't think it sounds at all like me." It would even be normal to develop a prejudice against such machines and to shun using them. Nevertheless, your recorded voice is the closest you will ever get to the voice that other people hear; and it is very close, as you will notice if you compare the live voices with the recorded voices of other people.

Initially, there will be a large amount of subjectivity in your listening to your own recorded voice. At first you will probably find it very difficult to credit your ears and accept the voice as your own. You may resist, rationalize, or even distort what you hear. For such resistance there are only two cures: (1) Wear it down through continued listening, and (2) keep listening until you have become well acquainted with your recorded voice. Whenever possible listen with someone by your side. Do not try at first to rate or evaluate your delivery. Seek merely to become accustomed to it.

We thus arrive at another principle. *If you want to improve your speaking, record your speech on a tape recorder and listen to what you have recorded.*

We cannot go much farther until the Voice Rating Sheet in Appendix A has been studied item by item. This is the subject of the next chapter. Before turning to this chapter, however, we should like to provide you with a practical encounter with the rating sheet.

Simply make several mimeographed copies of the Voice Rating Sheet and begin using it to evaluate the sermons and speeches of other people. (Wait a while to evaluate your own delivery!) In a class or workshop this means nothing more technical than a round of short talks with the whole class scoring each speaker in turn. Without a class, it means taking advantage of public meetings and radio and television speeches. Short-circuit for a time your usual habit of listening to *what* the speaker is saying and pay close attention to *how* he is saying it, taking up the items on the rating sheet a few at a time until each speech has been scored on each item. You probably will have a fair idea about the meaning of most of the items, but if you find yourself in doubt about any item, omit it from your scoring for the time being.

In this preliminary scoring you may feel very inexpert, but you will be educating your ear and you will also be sharpening your appetite for the discussion in the next chapter.

3. *What to Listen For*

If you have been following the suggestions presented, you have already used the Voice Rating Sheet in Appendix A for analyzing several speeches. You probably understand some of the factors on the rating scale but need additional information about others. Therefore, we stop at this point to anticipate and to answer several questions.

THE ITEMS ON THE RATING SHEET

Up to this point the vocal factors have been referred to rather generally as "the items on the rating sheet." Quality, pitch, inflection, rate, phrasing, and articulation are all parts of the oral communication pattern. They are not, however, static factors. Each element varies continuously, and the relationship among the elements keeps varying in an exceedingly complex manner. Thus the vocal factors are labeled *voice variables*. Since no two individuals use the voice variables in exactly the same way, their use constitutes what might be called an individual's *speech personality*.

The voice variables are in a functional sense secondary aspects of human speech. They are the "overlay" on the psychophysiological mechanisms which are the basic machinery of oral speech.

THE PSYCHOPHYSIOLOGICAL MECHANISMS OF SPEECH

Five psychophysiological activities are involved in the oral speech process: respiration, phonation, resonation, articulation, and inte-

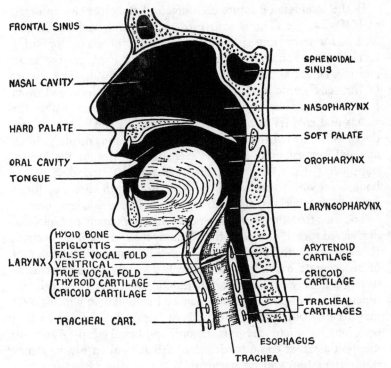

FRONTAL SINUS

NASAL CAVITY

HARD PALATE

ORAL CAVITY

TONGUE

SPHENOIDAL SINUS

NASOPHARYNX

SOFT PALATE

OROPHARYNX

LARYNGOPHARYNX

LARYNX
- HYOID BONE
- EPIGLOTTIS
- FALSE VOCAL FOLD
- VENTRICAL
- TRUE VOCAL FOLD
- THYROID CARTILAGE
- CRICOID CARTILAGE

ARYTENOID CARTILAGE

CRICOID CARTILAGE

TRACHEAL CART.

TRACHEAL CARTILAGES

ESOPHAGUS

TRACHEA

FIGURE 1.   Sagittal Section of Trachea, Larynx, Pharynx, Oral Cavity, and Nasal Cavity.

gration. These activities can be illustrated as follows. Breath is needed initially to get speech under way. Breath then passes through the adducted or partially adducted vocal cords in the larynx, and sound occurs. Sound is next resonated by various cavities in the mouth, throat, and nose. Then it is shaped into the consonants and vowels which form words by the major articulators—the tongue, teeth, and lips. Finally, the highly complex integration of all mechanisms occurs in the brain. Neural integration involves many psychological processes including audition, vision, symbolization, and thinking.

In the economy of nature each organ of speech is also an organ of biological life. The nose is used in breathing and smelling as well as for resonating speech. The teeth are necessary for biting and chewing, and the tongue for swallowing food; yet the teeth and tongue are also used for forming speech sounds. The closure of the vocal cords in the larynx helps to prevent food and other foreign matter from entering the trachea; their closure fixates the thorax and enables us to lift heavy objects. Yet the vibrations produced at the lips of the vocal cords result in sound. Breath is fundamental for sustaining life. The exchange of gases via the breathing process is a vital part of the biochemical functioning of our bodies. Yet we also use breath to speak. Finally, the brain performs a myriad of functions, of which the speaking process is only one.

The fact that the organs of speech are also organs of biological life has led speech specialists to call oral speech an *overlaid function*. It is important to keep this idea in mind because it is at the root of an accurate evaluation of a speech difficulty. It enables us to distinguish between *organic* and *functional* causes of speech disorders. For example, hoarseness may be functional, in which case it may result from excessive tension; or it may be organic, as it is occasionally where there is chronic postnasal drip. Again—to mention a rather common defect of articulation—a hissing *s* may result from the wrong placement of the tongue (functional) or it may be caused by the malformation of the teeth (organic), or a high-frequency hearing loss (also organic).

Some people are born with defective speech mechanisms like cleft palate or a hearing loss and begin life with an organically caused speech problem. Others, endowed with a normal machine, create an organic condition by misusing it. For example, speaking continuously at an unnaturally low pitch may develop a contact ulcer on the cords. On the other hand, it is well known that chronic hoarseness may be an early sign of cancer of the larynx. In cases where there is the slightest suspicion a medical check should be made.

It should be remembered while studying the voice variables that speech is an overlaid function and that the possibility of organic involvement does exist.

VOICE VARIABLES

1. *Pitch*

The first variable, pitch, must be considered along with phonation, which occurs in the larynx. The vocal folds are closed and tensed in various degrees as air passes through them. The result is sound.

The degree and tension of the closure, we believe, are largely the result of thoughts and feelings which are related to certain pitches. This process, however, happens so rapidly in the "mind's ear" that

FIGURE 2.   The Glottis During Phonation, Whispering, and Breathing.

we are seldom aware of it. Nevertheless, phonation mirrors us! It is in phonation that the following factors are shaped: pitch level, range (interval), intonation, and inflection.

The greatest enemy of proper phonation is abnormal tension. Poor mental hygiene is also an important factor. Usually the complex cure requires learning the art of relaxation as well as the insights of self-knowledge.

Pitch can be divided into a number of subfactors. From the Voice Rating Sheet it can be seen that pitch includes pitch level, range (interval), intonation, and inflection.

a. *Pitch level* is the first subfactor. For every mature human voice there is always a best pitch—best in the sense that it is most appropriate for that person's vocal machine. (We are talking about the voice after puberty, of course; it is not until the voice has finally changed that the situation for determining the best possible pitch occurs.)

Finding one's optimum pitch is not difficult for an individual with a good musical ear. The procedure is as follows. With the help of a piano, sing down the scale to the lowest note that you can comfortably sustain. Then go up the scale five semitones (five piano keys). That tone is usually the pitch around which you should speak most of the time. Most men find their optimum pitch at C below middle C on the piano, but others find it above or below that.

Determining optimum pitch for those who cannot carry a tune may be more difficult. One good way is to lie down comfortably and become as relaxed as possible. Then very easily, with no strain or excess effort, vocalize the *ah* sound as you emit a gentle sigh. (The whole sigh should be vocalized.) This sighing vowel should be at or very near your optimum pitch.

There is a strong tendency among men to speak below their optimum pitches. Probably because our culture seems to demand it, or because of the unspoken fear of "sounding like a sissy," many men cultivate the lower ranges of their voices. Higher pitches are traditionally associated with female voices. In addition to the strain on the vocal cords which may cause hoarseness, and possibly a contact ulcer, the practice of forcing one's pitch level down has another unhappy result: It limits the speaker's over-all range, causing him to use only the lower part of it and constricting him toward a monotone.

b. *Range* refers to the spread of one's speech in pitch both above and below his optimum pitch. The speaker who has a wide range and who uses it habitually will generally be more interesting than one whose range is more limited. One speaker experiencing great nervous excitement may pitch at a high level and neglect the bottom half of his range altogether. This is usually hard on the nerves and the ears of the listeners. Another may withdraw to the basement of his range and lull his listeners to sleep. The best voice is one making use of its full potential range, normally about an octave and a half.

Interval in speech, as in music, refers to the musical distance between two consecutive notes. The interval may come within a single word, or it may lie between two words. To experience the meaning of interval try saying "Hello" in a monotone at the bottom of your range. It sounds flat and unfriendly. Now say the same word, but speak the first syllable at a low pitch and then raise the second syllable about an octave above it: "Hel-LOW!" This will sound very enthusiastic, and very friendly. The distance between these two syllables is *interval*.

The same principle carries over into words within sentences. If all the words are spoken at the same pitch level, they will be hopelessly monotonous and dull. But if certain words are raised in pitch—if they have a wide interval from the preceding words— the monotony is broken and the speech becomes interesting. Interval suggests distinctions and contrasts of meaning. Almost every phrase spoken has certain key words that convey the meat of our thoughts; usually these key words are emphasized through the use of interval.

For illustration let us take a biblical quotation ("O Lord, thou hast searched me and known me") and mark it for interval. Marking the important key words, we might want to underscore *Lord*, *searched*, and *known*. Applying the principles mentioned, *O Lord* can be spoken at the bottom of the scale, and the words *searched* and *known* several tones above them. The other words can be said quickly, paying them little heed, and they will naturally fall somewhere in the middle, probably right at each speaker's optimum pitch. So diagrammed, the sentence looks like this:

<pre>
                SEARCHED   KNOWN
        thou hast   me, and   me."
"O LORD,
</pre>

Interval is thus used to single out important words. It may also be used to set words in contrast. If in a given sentence, for example, *darkness* is spoken in a low tone and *light* near the top of one's range, the interval between the two will show how opposite they are.

c. *Intonation* refers to a speaker's use of range in a specific sentence. Sometimes it is called *melody*. It means that a speaker's use of range is not haphazard but makes a tune. Normally we do not think about melody or intonation because it is a tune perfectly suited to the meaning, and also because it is the kind of thing we hear all around us in our region. Various national and regional speeches have their own melodies. Thus we quickly distinguish a Britisher from an American, a Pennsylvanian from a Texan. So intonation is determined partly by meaning and partly by custom.

The point at which melody gives trouble to preachers is in their tendency toward a stereotyped or patterned intonation. The tune is not suited to the meaning but is automatic and repetitive. This is called *ministerial tune*. It is not limited to ministers, however; professional politicians, college professors, and many other public speakers are as guilty of it as ministers. Curiously enough, it is usually a phenomenon that occurs only in public speeches. Private conversation is remarkably free of it. One difficulty in the way of overcoming it is that those who fall into it are seldom aware of it. Here is one point at which a recorder and an assistant listener are indispensable.

d. *Inflection* is a glide within one syllable of a word or in a word of one syllable by which we express conviction, doubt, sarcasm, question, and a number of other attitudes. Perhaps the best way of getting at it is to illustrate. Speak the following capitalized words in such a manner as to convey the meaning described in parenthesis:

GO HOME (Oh, leave, will you?)
GO HOME (Right this minute!)
GO HOME (Pleading: come on, it's best if you do.)
GO HOME (Why should I?)
GO HOME (Are you serious? I have no home.)

GO HOME (Are you telling me what to do?)
GO HOME (Yes, that's just what I want to do.)[1]

An analysis of your reading of each statement will show that you probably used three different kinds of inflections: downward, upward, and circumflex. To these the flat inflection should be added. Generally in our culture inflections are used in the following ways: downward, for strong affirmation; upward, for questions; circumflex, for a variety of mixed emotions like doubt and sarcasm; and flat, for disappointment or disgust.

Obviously inflections are an important index to a speaker's feelings. It is not the words themselves but the inflections that carry the real emotional meaning. For example, one can say, "Where are you going?" and have it mean two opposite things just by changing the inflection. With a rising inflection it expresses simple interest. Yet when spoken with a strong downward inflection it expresses stubborn opposition and actually means, "Stay right here!"

As with intonation, inflection becomes very important in public speaking because it may fall into a stereotype. A consistently heavy downward inflection may convey the impression of pugnacity. A consistently rising inflection will give the impression of being undecided, tentative. Almost always a ministerial tune will include an inflection pattern. Some factors in addition to intonation and inflection, however, are involved in ministerial tune. We shall therefore return to this topic later.

2. Quality

In order to understand voice quality it is necessary first to explore the principles of resonation.

Sound initiated at the vocal cords is relatively colorless. It needs to be amplified and reinforced to provide pleasant quality. Just as violin strings need expertly hollowed wood to give mellowness, so the vocal cords need their resonators. The major speech resona-

[1] Adapted from Thomas V. Liske, *Effective Preaching* (Macmillan: 1951), p. 67.

tors are the cavities of the throat, nose, and mouth and any of their divisions.

The performance of any resonator is dependent on four factors: (1) volume, (2) shape, (3) degree of opening, and (4) texture of the surfaces. The human resonators are no exceptions. You may discover this easily by phonating the vowel *u* as in *who* with your lips barely open. Then phonate the same vowel again with your lips rounded into a pucker. You will notice the sharp contrast in the sound which occurs. This difference is caused by the change in the mouth cavity which your lips have provided.

Although the human resonators are limited by their basic bony structure, they are nevertheless very adaptable. It has already been seen how the lips are related to resonation. The tongue is equally important. We need only to phonate *e* as in *see* and then *o* as in *so* to observe again the marked change occurring inside the mouth cavity as a result of the tongue's action.

Each of us seems to have a habitual way of resonating, and because of this, a distinctive sound or voice quality. Two individuals, for example, might repeat identical sentences using the same pitch, inflection, rate, etc., yet we could still tell without looking that one was Mr. X and the other Mr. Y.

This distinctiveness is probably due largely to individual differences in the basic physiological resonators; however, this factor does not appear to limit the extent to which they may be used. We are all familiar with mimics who have mastered the art of imitation. They prove one point: not only the resonators but the entire speech apparatus is extremely flexible. Of course, we may not all be as skillful as the professional impersonators, but, by understanding and using the human resonators efficiently, we can greatly improve our voice quality.

Research[2] by one of the authors has demonstrated that certain aspects of voice quality are not liked by the average listener. Breathiness, nasality, harshness, and hoarseness were given unfavorable

[2] Charles F. Diehl and Eugene T. McDonald, "Effect of Voice Quality on Communication," *Journal of Speech and Hearing Disorders*, June, 1956, pp. 233-237.

ratings by listeners, whereas a voice free from these characteristics was given an excellent rating.

We shall think, therefore, of superior voice quality as being free of breathiness, nasality, harshness, and hoarseness. A description of these four follows:

a. *Breathiness* is usually the cause when speech sounds like half-whisper and half-voice. Characteristic, too, are audible gulpings for breath, and phrases interrupted in meaningless ways. Emphasis seems almost uniform throughout. The general impression is one of low vitality—almost lethargy. Breathiness is generally the result of insufficient closure of the opening between the vocal folds. Too much unphonated air is permitted to escape. This air generates its own peculiar noisy sound. The resonating cavities are consequently rendered less efficient as the excessive air dampens the speech sounds that would normally be resonated.

Some research has indicated that there is a distinct relationship between breathiness and introversion. Fearful of expressing himself, the shy, withdrawn individual half-talks, half-whispers. With others, of course, breathiness may be purely the result of poor breathing and speaking habits.

b. *Nasality* occurs when normally oral sounds are allowed to issue through the nose. The back part of the roof of the mouth is called the soft palate. In many ways it is comparable to a trap door between the nose and the mouth. For all speech sounds except *m*, *n*, and *ng* the soft palate normally is elevated and almost touches the throat wall. This partition thus serves to divert the sounds out through the mouth. For *m*, *n*, and *ng* the soft palate hangs down normally in its relaxed position, permitting the sounds to travel out through the nose. For most people, the appropriate action for the various sounds occurs almost involuntarily as the result of habit. For others, environmental factors or improper speech habits have delayed the normal action.

Two major kinds of deviations interfere with normal resonation: hypernasality and hyponasality.

Hypernasality means the resonation of nonnasal sounds in the nasal cavities. Cleft palate or a foreshortened soft palate are organic causes of hypernasality requiring the assistance of trained specialists. Yet a great deal of hypernasality is entirely functional. In certain regions of the country it is characteristic. In parts of Texas, New Jersey, New England, and Kentucky vowels are normally nasalized by arching the tongue high in the back of the mouth. Sounds are consequently directed up and out through the nose.

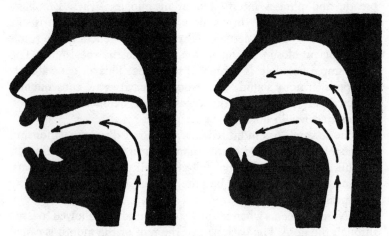

FIGURE 3. The Mouth, Nasal Passage, and Pharynx During the Production of Nasal and Oral Sounds. Note that with the velum raised, the speech is largely oral; but with the velum lowered the speech is nasalized.

If doubt exists as to what hypernasality sounds like, try humping your tongue high in the middle. Retract it backwards slightly with considerable tension, then say "How are you?" You will notice that the phrase seems to be coming from your nose rather than your mouth. Ear training is basic for overcoming hypernasality. One must learn to hear in others and in himself the difference between a sound that is resonated nasally and one that is resonated orally.

During nasal resonance the vibrations in the nose can be felt.

During oral resonance they cannot. These physical sensations should be used as additional clues in evaluating voice quality. (See Appendix C, pp. 147-148.)

Hyponasality refers to a lack of nasal resonation even for those sounds normally resonated exclusively in the nose (*m, n, ng*).

When one has a severe head cold, he will have a cold-in-the-head sound. This is hyponasality. The nasal passages are congested and prevent normal sound passage through them.

Chronic hyponasality is usually caused by congestions, malformations, enlarged adenoids, and other organic conditions. It can rarely be eliminated without medical intervention.

c. *Harshness* is the third characteristic likely to be rated unfavorably. If an individual speaks in a vacant room containing no carpets or curtains his voice quality will sound quite sharp, almost metallic. In the same room, however, with several people, furniture, carpeting, and draperies his voice quality will probably sound more mellow. This difference occurs as a result of a resonation principle—that surface texture of resonators is very important for the quality of the tones produced by them.

The empty room acted as a resonator for the voice. Since there were in the room no hangings, coverings, or clothing of other individuals to soften its surfaces, the sounds introduced into it literally bounced off the bare, hard walls and floor. No mellowing of the tones was possible.

The same principle holds for the human resonators. If there is excessive tension and constriction in the throat and mouth the surfaces of those areas will, as a result, be drawn tight. Tones passing through them will be sharply reflected in much the same way as in the empty room. The quality resulting from tense surfaces is generally called *harsh*. It can be overcome by first training the ear to recognize it. Then with appropriate relaxation, proper breathing, and healthy mental attitude, adequate use of the resonators can be made.

d. *Hoarseness* may be chronic or acute. Most of us at one time or another have had laryngitis or a severe cough. When we speak during these periods our voices have a husky, strained, gravel-like sound—a *hoarseness*. Some people sound this way constantly with or without laryngitis.

Chronic hoarseness, as has been mentioned previously, should not be taken lightly. A medical check by a reliable ear, nose, and throat specialist is always the first step in its evaluation.

Hoarseness may have many causes. Perhaps the most common is speaking constantly below one's optimum pitch with a very narrow range. Why this is such a common cause is not clear; however, some cases at least are the result of imitation of established public performers whose low, throaty quality is considered an asset. For others, strong feelings of insecurity have led to an unnaturally low pitch, associated apparently with "maturity," "masculinity," and "authority."

Among organic causes of chronic hoarseness are contact ulcer, vocal nodules, nerve paralysis, allergies, and carcinoma. Trained specialists should always be consulted in remedial programs involving any of these.

If there is no organic pathology to consider, the establishment of optimum pitch is basic to overcoming hoarseness (see p. 20). Since excessive tension is frequently a factor, proper relaxation is essential. Evaluation of self-concepts may be very critical to recovery. It is important, too, to remember the principle of resonation—that even a high-pitched voice will sound rich and clear if it is properly resonated with adequate breath support. (See Appendix C, pp. 146-147).

3. *Articulation*

Not to be confused with diction or pronunciation, articulation is synonymous with enunciation. It is the formation of resonated tone into the vowels and consonants of connected speech largely by means of the tongue, teeth, and lips. It is a highly complex activity calling for great flexibility and mobility of these structures and for an educated ear. There are roughly half a hundred different sounds in American speech. Few people articulate all of them equally well.

Each of the fifty sounds may be misarticulated in four ways.

Sounds may be (1) omitted, as in *guvmen* (government); (2) distorted, as in *faht* (fight); (3) substituted for, as in *gineration* (generation); improperly voiced like *lives or words* (livz, wordz—the final *s* should be sounded as a *z*); or (4) added, as in *idear* (idea).

To understand the process of articulation better, speak a word and then analyze the processes. Take the simple word *bus*. To produce that word it is necessary to articulate three sounds. First, we put the lips together and voice the *b*; then, quickly we open

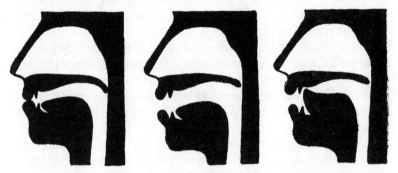

FIGURE 4.   Lips, Tongue, and Velum during the Articulation of *Bus*.

the mouth a little, arch the tongue slightly in the middle and voice *uh*; and we finish by almost closing the teeth, grooving the tongue slightly anchoring the two front corners of the tongue against the upper teeth ridge (just back of and at the base of the upper teeth), and pointing the tip of the tongue upward slightly but without touching anything—holding that position we blow a gentle unvoiced breath, and we are saying *s*. If we voice the last sound (*s*) it will become *z*, and the word will then be *buz* instead of *bus*.

All of this to say *bus!* It can be spoken in an instant, yet a full minute is required to describe the process. From what has been said, however, it should not be difficult to see how easy it is to make a mistake in articulation. Consider the word *bus* again. Some people

say *bud* instead; others say *bush* or *buth*. These are errors of substitution. Some people, in a quickly spoken sentence will say *bu*,
making an error of omission. Many will say the final *s* with an
undue hissing or whistling sound; this is a distortion. Trouble with
the *s* sound is so common that this particular distortion has been
given its own name, sigmatism. In some southern regions people
say *bu us*, adding a second, though shorter *uh* sound in the middle
of the word. This is an example of addition.

In rough phonetic transcription there are fifty symbols of American speech. Each of these can be spoken with four different kinds
of mistake. This means that we are capable of no less than 200
different errors of articulation!

But in actual practice it is never as bad as that. A given individual
tends to have only a few articulation errors, like sigmatism (hissing
s), making *ng*'s into *n*'s or substituting one vowel for another. He
repeats these over and over, but with a little attention to his
peculiar problems he can be articulating quite normally in a matter
of weeks.

Many speakers never fully realize that their own articulation is
faulty until they hear themselves on a tape recording. Then they
become concerned and self-critical. But they do not know what
to do about it. Given a strong motivation—a real desire to improve—any man working to better his articulation will have three
things to do:

a. He must achieve more flexibility in the physical organs of
articulation; i.e., tongue, lips, and jaw muscles must become more
active and more agile. To be clear, the sounds of speech have to be
shaped, with a definite, clear-cut position of all the articulators
for each one of the fifty sounds of American English. Many people,
even professional speakers, have lazy tongues, and lips and jaws
that are almost immobile. Some clamp the teeth nearly shut as if
to imprison every word that is uttered.

Exercises for the flexing of the chief articulators may be found
in Appendix C of this book, pp. 152-153.

b. He must educate the muscles of the mouth until he can feel
the correct position as against the incorrect position for the sounds

he is working to improve. Since this involves for most men no more than half a dozen sounds, it is really not very difficult. But it is important to learn the proper sound through the proper motor impressions from within the mouth. One reason a sound is produced incorrectly is that it is firmly lodged in a motor habit; it "feels" right, even though it may sound wrong on a tape recording. For some mysterious reason, what a man "feels" in his mouth as he speaks seems to overrule his ears; and he actually fails to hear his mistakes while he is talking. By the same token, in the re-education of the articulators, the proper position for the producing of a sound long misarticulated will seem strange and unnatural at first. This unnatural feeling has to be overcome by habit—which means frequent repetition—and by mental reassurance, which comes from listening to tape recordings of the improvement as it is made.

For example, to use a minor illustration, suppose a man has been saying *hep* and we ask him to say *help* instead. He can say it correctly, but it "feels" exaggerated and unnatural; he is afraid to say it as *help* for fear he will be thought affected. To give him the needed mental reassurance we ask him to read a sentence containing the word into the tape recorder, saying it both ways. Then, as he listens to it when it is played back, he will realize that the correct pronunciation sounds "right." He can then go on to re-educate his tongue, and before long *hep* will be gone from his vocabulary forever.

There is yet one more thing a speaker must do to improve articulation:

c. He must sharpen his hearing. Re-education of tongue and ear go together, as we have just indicated—ear helping tongue and tongue helping ear. The simplest method is to work with a companion from another region, isolating the incorrect sounds and repeating the words and phrases containing them, alternating between right and wrong until the differences can be clearly recognized.

For example, many speakers in southeastern United States say *min* (men), *gineration* (generation), *siminary* (seminary), *miny* (many). They require some little practice before they begin to feel and hear the vowel substitution of which they are guilty; but until they do hear it they cannot go forward. Here again, a tape recorder is an invaluable aid; and a fellow listener is indispensable.

A speaker who wants to master the articulation of all sounds of American speech should learn and use the International Phonetic Alphabet. A teacher is not required. A conscientious use of *Good American Speech* by Margaret McLean (Dutton, 1952) or of *An*

FIGURE 5.   Positions of the Tongue in Resonating Front and Back Vowels. Position at left is for *u* as in *who*; position at right is for *e* as in *me*.

Introduction to General American Phonetics by Charles Van Riper and Dorothy Smith (Harper, 1954) will put phonetics within the grasp of any interested person in a matter of weeks. Also see Appendix C, VIII, D, "Acquiring and Using the Phonetic Alphabet," pp. 157-163.

There is, however, a simpler way of improving one's articulation. This method attacks only the sounds which a given person misarticulates. Here it is, step by step:

Step 1. Record a speech, sermon, or reading—preferably from a "live" situation. For ministers, this may mean a recording from a regular church service and will include the full sermon.

Step 2. With "assistant listeners" by your side, play back the tape, writing a list of all mispronounced and misarticulated words. If some of your fellow listeners are from a region other than your own, so much the better. Let them help in the list making.

Step 3. Classify your mistakes. For example, one man may find that he habitually distorts the diphthongs: *ai* as in *sky* (skah), *high* (hah), and *oi* as in *boy* (baw), *oil* (awl). He may also drop many of his middle *t*'s and *d*'s, as in *handle* (han'le) and *sentence* (sen'ence). A classification of the words which he misarticulates will show, therefore, that he can cure his difficulties if he masters the proper articulation of four sounds: two diphthongs and two consonants.

Step 4. Work directly to correct the offending vowels, diphthongs, and consonants which step 3 has located. There are two different ways of doing this: (a) The simplest method is to buy and use the long-playing records of *The Speechphone Method—Speech Sounds and Rhythms of American English* (Intermediate Course), produced by Linguaphone Institute, 30 Rockefeller Plaza, New York 20, N.Y. The recording is done by Hazel P. Brown and it is accompanied by a printed manual. The records provide a separate band and lesson for each speech sound. The method of each lesson is based on listening and repeating words, phrases, and sentences. Each lesson starts with precise directions for placing the mouth, tongue, and lips to produce the sound under study. With an assistant listener (or a tape recorder) it will be possible to compare Miss Brown's correct articulation with your own and to work until you have matched it.

This step isolates speech sounds and enables you to work on one at a time. You learn the correct position in the mouth and match your articulation against a standard spoken by another voice. You form new oral habits and acquire a keener ear for each sound. And you repeat until you have it firmly in mind.

(b) A second way of practicing correct articulation of offending sounds is to follow the exercises on pp. 153-156 in this book. Here we have dealt with the sounds most commonly giving trouble. For other sounds we recommend the phonetic method, through the books and exercises already mentioned above. You will need someone to work with you and help you listen. A tape recording will also help.

Step 5. You now practice speaking these sounds in the words, phrases, and sentences which you normally use. One way of doing this is to take your list of words and phrases from step 2 and, using it, underscore these same words and phrases in the manuscript of your sermon. A moment's reflection will show you that it is relatively easy to speak the new sounds correctly as long as they are isolated and appear in single words. It is considerably more difficult to speak them correctly in rapidly moving phrases, where they appear in company with numerous other sounds. Repeat these words and phrases over and over until you have overcome your old speech habits for the time being. And keep returning to such repetition for successive sermons.

Step 6. Watch yourself in your daily conversation and, when politeness permits, correct yourself on the spot at the time you are talking. It is the daily habits of speech that carry over into the pulpit. And we do not want you to acquire two ways of talking, one for private consumption, the other for public ears. What you incorporate into daily speech is what you will carry with you as you stand up to speak.

The six steps which we have just outlined will carry you, if you practice them, directly to General American Speech. Two words of warning need to be sounded: Don't get discouraged if you do not register spectacular gains quickly; an old habit has to be eradicated and a new one established. This requires time. Again, avoid pedantic over-articulation. The sounds of speech must flow together. Moreover, many of them appear in weaker and stronger forms. For example, we should not say, "Thee boy went to thee town." Rather we should say, "Thuh boy went tuh thuh town" (speaking *thuh* and *tuh* quickly and lightly). There are about forty words that appear in these weaker forms. A list is given in the exercises on pp. 156-157.

To summarize: Locate the offending sounds in your speech, learn to feel and to hear these sounds when correctly produced, practice them separately and in connected speech, and keep on repeating them day by day until you have mastered them.

4. Pronunciation

Pronunciation is not to be confused with articulation. It refers to the accenting of syllables within a word. For example, we do not say *a-muse*-MENT, stressing the last syllable. We say *a*-MUSE-*ment*, stressing the second. A dictionary will indicate the accepted syllable stress for any word.

(*Diction* has nothing to do with articulation or pronunciation. It refers only to the choice of words. For example, X might say, "The speaker was witty," while Y might say, "The speaker was humorous." Both mean the same thing. The difference in word choice is a difference in their diction.)

5. Rate

Rate refers to the speed with which we speak. Studies have been made to determine the best over-all rate of speech, but the findings have shown only that there is considerable variation among those who are recognized as good speakers. Rate is defective only if it is so fast as to hinder understanding or so slow as to cause boredom.

One of the most important elements of good rate is flexibility. A good speaker keeps changing pace every few seconds. Suppose we take a quotation from the scripture to illustrate the point.

"But he, desiring to justify himself, said to Jesus, 'And who is my neighbor?' Jesus replied, 'A man was going down from Jerusalem to Jericho, and he fell among robbers, who stripped him, and beat him, and departed, leaving him half dead.'" (Luke 10: 29-30.)

When we examine that quotation phrase by phrase, marking each phrase for the speed at which it should be spoken, we may get something like this:

MODERATE:	"But he,
FAST:	desiring to justify himself,
MODERATE:	said to Jesus,

SLOW:	'And who is my neighbor?'
FAST:	Jesus replied,
MODERATE:	'A man was going down from Jerusalem to Jericho,
SLOW:	and he fell among robbers,
SLOW:	who stripped him,
SLOW:	and beat him,
SLOW:	and departed,
SLOW:	leaving him half dead.' "

Actually, speech is even more flexible than we have just indicated. For within some of the slow phrases certain words are spoken more slowly still. Such words as *Jerusalem, Jericho, robbers, beat,* and *half dead* are elongated. Normally, we have a great deal of flexibility and change of pace in everyday conversation but when we get up to read or make a speech we tend to become wooden and less flexible. Whenever a speech sounds as if it were recited or read, it probably lacks flexibility.

With all the change in pace suggested, it should be remembered that good speaking *flows*. It has *fluency*. In general this refers to readiness of speech, to the absence of hesitations, and the suiting of rate to meanings.

One form of non-fluency is the verbalized pause which appears as *uh, ah,* or *um*. Even the most skilled speakers occasionally use a verbalized pause. Used excessively, however, verbalized pauses are very distressing to listeners. Unfortunatelly, a speaker seldom realizes when he has this habit. The cure for him is to listen to a tape recording of his speech until he becomes familiar with his pause pattern. He can then work toward improvement.

Another form of non-fluency is the lurching delivery of pauses that are prolonged or misplaced. This may come from poor preparation, or from an impoverished vocabulary; or it may come from *staccato phonation*—a habitual shortening of vowels plus a machine-gun-like spitting out and running together of syllables. A speaker who does this talks faster than he can think, so he stumbles and hesitates between thoughts. (For exercises to overcome staccato phonation see Appendix C, pp. 153-156.

6. *Loudness*

Loudness refers to the amount of force needed to deliver the spoken word to those who are listening. It must be loud enough to be heard with ease, even on the back pew, but not loud enough to bombard the listeners. A speaker is often a poor judge of his own volume. One is so quiet we have to strain to hear him; another is so loud we recoil from the impact. Still another leaps from one extreme to the other—now shouting, now whispering—an imaginative observer has called this kind of speaker "the cliff-jumper."

Loudness has to be suited to the hall and to the situation, and it has to be learned. Since a speaker may not be his own best judge in this respect, it would be wise for him to have one or two people in the audience check his volume from time to time. Unfortunately, the tape recorder under ordinary conditions is no help here; the microphone (which may be considered a mechanical ear) is within inches as we record. Moreover, the volume of the tape recorder is so adjustable that a man playing back his own sermon has no way by himself of knowing what volume matches his own.

With the help of a discerning friend it is possible, however, to hear your own volume. The method is to place the recorder on the pulpit and have a friend to adjust the volume—going back and forth from his customary seat in the pews—until he has it at your usual level. You, meantime, should be seated in the sanctuary well toward the back. Speakers accused of too little volume will learn a great deal from this method, perhaps more than those who are too loud.

Loudness is important for audibility, but variations of loudness are also used for emphasizing important ideas. Key words and phrases are usually spoken with a slight increase in volume. *Emphasis* is thus related to loudness.

It should be remembered, however, that emphasis does not depend on volume alone. Emphasis is distorted if attempted solely by increasing or decreasing loudness. The effect is that of the "cliff-jumper" whom we met a moment ago. So, if accused of whispering or shouting to get important ideas across, try speaking weightier phrases and words *more slowly*. Emphasis may be achieved through a combination of slowing the rate and only slightly increasing the loudness. It may also be achieved by pausing after or before an important word or phrase.

7. *Phrasing*

A phrase is a series of words representing a unit of thought. Usually, we communicate thoughts in phrases rather than by individual words. To separate our thoughts and to show how they are connected or contrasted with each other, we use pauses. So *phrasing* and *pausing* go together. To be meaningful a speech needs a great deal of well-placed silence.

Not all pauses are alike. Some are brief, almost tentative. Others may be very long if there is a marked shift in ideas; then the pause acts as a kind of curtain to close a scene. And there are pauses of intermediate length. In conversation we pause spontaneously and meaningfully, but in public speech and even more in public reading we may tend to shorten and to equalize our pauses, robbing our expression of its rightful variety and freshness. It sounds paradoxical, but in assessing a speech we need to listen to the pauses. One of the most revealing things we can do is to record a scrap of our ordinary conversation and then compare it with a part of our recorded public speeches, giving special attention to the pauses in it.

Pauses can be misplaced, in which cases there are hesitations rather than genuine pauses. Then the phrases they punctuate are broken and the thought of the speech loses clarity and persuasiveness.

Errors in phrasing and pausing may be overcome by studying a manuscript and marking it for logical thought groupings and points of emphasis. In Chapter 8 this procedure is discussed in detail.

It should be realized that emphasis is related to phrasing. In every phrase there is at least one accented word, just as there is one accented syllable in every word. Thus, what we have already said about emphasis and flexibility of *range* or *interval* applies here too. That is to say, the emphasized word is spoken a little more loudly than other words, a little more slowly, and with a pitch interval between itself and its neighbors. In general, the wider the interval the more animated and natural speech sounds. We come here to a rather surprising rule: *Exaggeration* (if not outlandish or extreme) *increases naturalness*.

CONCLUSION

This completes the survey of the voice variables listed on the Voice Rating Sheet on p. 133. For purposes of analysis the variables have been separated. Yet it should be remembered that in living speech the variables are united into an interrelated whole and rooted in the total personality of the speaker. (This relationship will be discussed in Chapter 7: "What Are You Saying Emotionally?") A purely mechanical approach to isolated speech problems, therefore, is almost always inadequate. When a deviation in one of the voice variables is discovered, one should first ask why it is there, and then begin work at the root causes. It should be remembered, too, that several separate deviations may not really be separate: they may form a cluster with a common rootage. For example, if a speaker's will to communicate is weak, this basic defect may be reflected in several places on the rating scale: in too little volume, in poor emphasis, and in a general monotony which shows up both in rate and pitch. Usually it is wise to treat an adverse reading on the rating sheet as a symptom, and to look beyond the symptom for the parent difficulty.

4.   Foundations of Effective Voice

A large number of speech problems can be solved by developing appropriate speech breathing habits plus optimal relaxation. Defects of quality, especially breathiness, harshness, and hoarseness as well as insufficient loudness, poor phrasing, and emphasis are cases in point. Those who have any of these problems, and even those who do not, will profit considerably by emphasizing and developing these fundamentals of speech—breathing and relaxation. They are basic to the delivery of any effective speaker.

BREATHING FOR SPEECH

Anyone who has not worked on proper breathing under an instructor at some earlier time may have a little difficulty at first in getting the matter in hand. The trouble usually stems from the fact that there are two markedly different kinds of breathing—one for biological needs and the other for speech. One difference between breathing for metabolism and breathing for speech is in the contrasting rhythm. For metabolism it goes like this: Inhale through the nose (1-2-3); exhale through the nose (1-2-3). But in speech it should go like this: Inhale through the mouth (1); exhale through the mouth (1-2-3-4-5-6-7). Of course, in speech there is no exact mathematical ratio, but when a person is talking he has to inhale quickly and let the breath expire slowly and rather evenly while vibrating the vocal cords. Whereas breathing for metabolism is involuntary, breathing for speech has to be voluntarily controlled.

Since we cannot ordinarily inhale while actually emitting tone, during speech we have to inhale quickly in the pauses between phrases. This limitation—the shortness of the time for inhaling—may foster the habit of taking a shallow breath insufficient to last for the phrase that follows it. Then the only way to speak a phrase

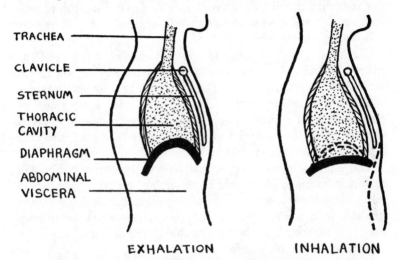

TRACHEA

CLAVICLE

STERNUM

THORACIC
CAVITY

DIAPHRAGM

ABDOMINAL
VISCERA

EXHALATION   INHALATION

FIGURE 6.   Diaphragmatic Breathing. Diagram showing how the downward contraction of the diaphragm increases the size of the thoracic cavity, decreasing the air pressure within the thorax and permitting the inflow of air from outside the body. Note also that this movement displaces the abdominal viscera downward and forward, causing the abdomen to be enlarged as much as, or more than, the chest.

is either to croak out its last syllables with a straining throat or to interrupt the phrase in a frantic gasp for the air required to finish it.

Something else may also happen. A speaker may breathe somewhat after the manner of an athlete about to have his chest expansion measured. To experience this kind of breathing, do the following: Place your right palm against your diaphragm and take a deep breath in such a way as to expand your chest to its greatest girth. You will notice that your right hand was not forced out; if anything it may have been sucked in slightly. Your diaphragm, in other words, was practically inactive. In the meantime, you lifted your rib cage from the top. If you were standing before a mirror you saw your shoulders lift at the same time. As you can see, this process involves the shoulders or clavicles, and that is why it is frequently called clavicular breathing.

Clavicular breathing tends to constrict the entire region of the throat. It creates tension both in the larynx and in the throat cavities which resonate tones. The result will be a constricted tone, a tired throat, and a harsh or hoarse voice—plus a great deal of fatigue after the completion of a speech. Some people have fallen into the habit of breathing this way, and they have used it so long that it seems entirely natural for them.

The establishment of appropriate speech breathing habits will require retraining. The period of retraining, necessarily, will be a self-conscious one, in which breathing-for-speech will seem "unnatural" for a while. What we propose to do, however, is to keep breathing-for-speech as close as possible to the easy and automatic way in which we breathe-for-life.

Before you begin working at this for yourself, you may want to check the following common errors against your own habits:

Wrong: Glottal shock, a violent eruption of sound at the beginning of words, sentences, and phrases, is caused by stopping and releasing the breath with the closing and opening of the vocal cords. Breath is inhaled, built up in pressure behind the vocal cords, and exhaled with an initial explosion.

Correct: The air is taken in easily through the mouth without gulping and released smoothly through the vocal cords during vocalization. The process should call no attention to itself.

Wrong: During inhalation the rib cage is noticeably lifted by elevating the clavicles and sternum toward the chin. The larynx housing the vocal cords is constricted downward. This is called clavicular breathing.

Correct: The diaphragm does most of the work. By its action this powerful muscle dividing the thorax from the abdomen compresses the viscera outward and forces the rib cage up and out. The process is scarcely noticeable, provides more control, and eliminates constriction at the vocal cords and surrounding resonators. It is called diaphragmatic breathing.

RELAXATION

Before a person can work directly on breathing with full satisfaction, he must learn how to relax. Perhaps we had better say it another way, for "Relax!" sounds like a call to action. The word suggests effort, and effort calls for some muscle tension. What we want to do, on the contrary, is to eliminate muscle tension; so it is more helpful to say, "Let go!" It is negative effort that we are calling for. We want to learn how to let all muscles sag, to let go completely.

The best way to learn when a muscle is relaxed is first to become aware of it when it is very tense. So begin by tensing your muscles, but do this progressively, in the following manner: With a friend or classmate helping to check your compliance with the instructions, begin by lying down, flat on your back. (The floor is as good a place as any, but a couch or bed will do.)

First, raise your right arm about four inches from the floor and stretch it to the finger tips as tightly as you possibly can, until you actually begin to feel a little pain. Increase the tension until the muscles are quivering. Now let go; let the right arm slump to the floor in exhaustion.

Second, with knee unbent, raise your right foot an inch or two from the floor, point your toes, and tense all the muscles of your right leg until you are quivering with the effort. At the same time lift your right arm as before and tense it also. Hold this rigid position for about a minute; then drop both arm and leg to the floor, releasing all the muscles simultaneously.

Third, tense your right arm as before, but release the tension only in certain muscle groups, one at a time, as your friend or classmate calls them off, in the following order: fingers, wrist, elbow, shoulder, and whole arm. The important thing is to be aware of the contrast between tension and relaxation from your shoulder to the tips of your fingers. This ultimately will teach you to check your body lying down, standing, or sitting, and—even under pressure—to determine which muscle groups are excessively tense.

Fourth, continue by thinking of muscle groups in other parts of your body—abdomen, chest, shoulders, neck, throat, and forehead. Begin from a condition of universal tenseness, making sure that you have pulled your shoulders up and in toward your neck and that you have drawn your brow into a deep frown. Then progressively let the muscle groups go, moving from the fingers up each arm, and from the toes up each leg in turn; go on to the shoulders, and neck, to the jaw muscles, the throat, and the forehead. At the end of the exercise you will lie exhausted, little more than a sack of flesh and bones—relaxed in every part of your body.

Fifth (to see how tension relates to your vocal mechanism), sit upright in a chair and tense all the muscles in the area of your throat. Pull your shoulders up to your neck. Pull your chin down against your chest. Lift your whole rib cage. Where do you feel the most tension? Probably in your throat. Suppose you had to speak through such tension! Of course the tension is exaggerated, yet it is only a matter of degree. There are many speakers who squeeze out their voices under great tension.

Someone may object that complete relaxation is more conducive to sleeping than to speaking. The objection is well taken. Actually, the relaxation exercises above are preliminary to speaking; their aim is to free a speaker of excessive tension so that his body will respond quickly and flexibly to his changing ideas. For the speech situation itself it is not complete relaxation but tonus that is required. Tonus is that delicate balance of tension and relaxation—neither too much nor too little—appropriate for what has to be done.

The exercises in progressive relaxation just outlined should be practiced regularly, day after day for a few minutes. The process is not quite as simple as we have made it, but we have applied the big brush strokes and examined the main features. More detailed instructions for relaxation are outlined in Appendix C, pp. 144-145. Anyone who cares to study relaxation more thoroughly should read *You Must Relax*, by Edmund Jacobsen (McGraw-Hill, 1942).

DIAPHRAGMATIC BREATHING

It will be seen at once that diaphragmatic breathing ties in with relaxation. Breathing from the diaphragm is a way of breathing that reduces muscle tension in the throat area. This is very important.

Yet diaphragmatic breathing does something more than relax throat tensions and open up the tone passages. It also gives an adequate air supply and provides an easy means of control. The best way to understand this is to do the following exercises:

First, lie down on a hard surface on the flat of your back, as at the beginning of the relaxation exercises. Tense all your muscles as before and progressively let them go in groups as before until you lie completely relaxed. You will feel tired and sleepy.

Second, remaining as limp as possible, have a friend or a classmate place his right palm over your diaphragm, just above your belt line and just below your short ribs, letting it rest there without applying pressure. Say nothing; merely breathe as nature lets you, sleepily and without effort. You will be aware of your friend's hand riding up and down in response to the action of your diaphragm. Your shoulders will not move. Your lungs will fill as if from the bottom. Breathing will by rhythmical and effortless. This is breathing-for-life, and it is diaphragmatic, as you can see.

Third, with a friend or classmate helping you as before, use one of your exhalations to emit a deep, sleepy sigh. All the breathing action should be from your diaphragm, as in the second step.

Fourth, repeat the third step, but this time vocalize the sigh, saying the vowel *ah* as in *father*. Do it lazily, and say nothing but the vocalized sigh. Your tone will be very breathy, little more than a whisper.

Fifth, repeat with this difference: Now you want this single tone to be heard twenty to forty feet away. You will have to inhale more quickly and emit your breath more slowly. Your tone should be clear and strong. Repeat this several times, your friend checking all the while to make sure that you are doing it all with your diaphragm and not moving your shoulders.

Sixth, continue the same kind of exercise using other vowels and diphthongs. Just to make sure that you have an open tone, put an *h* before these vowels, like *ha, ho, how, he, hoi, hi,* and so on. Produce these sounds separately, one to a breath. All you have to do is to change the shape of your lips for the different sounds; everything else is the same.

You will soon become more aware of how sounds are formed. One good way to think of the vowel is to envision it perching in the middle of your tongue just before you gently guide it out through your lips. Let it float out.

Have your friend keep checking on your breathing. You should be inhaling for every breath group, using your diaphragm but not your shoulders. When inhaling, your diaphragm should force his hand away from you; when speaking syllables, your diaphragm should be collapsing, like a balloon from which the air is being allowed to escape in short bursts. Do not thrust the diaphragm out while you are emitting tone, but only to draw breath in.

To connect diaphragmatic breathing with speech we must go beyond single vowels to words and phrases. To speak, we must take in a breath quickly through the mouth (without gulping) and use it up slowly as we utter a phrase. Recall what was said on p. 40 about the ratio of inhaling and exhaling. The idea in speaking is to conserve breath through several words, until a natural pause is reached. Then after replenishing your air supply proceed in the same manner, speaking a few words and taking a new breath as long as you are talking. After major pauses exhale completely and take in a completely new breath before speaking the next phrase. At minor pauses, however, do not exhale at all; merely inhale to replenish your air supply. It is important to maintain a full supply of air.

Seventh, to get the feeling of speaking in breath groups, group vowel sounds, like this: Inhale; say *ha, ho, how* on one breath.

Then exhale, and repeat, using various vowel sounds combined with consonants. Gradually increase the number of sounds emitted on one breath.

Eighth, using the same techniques, begin to speak short sentences, still lying prone. The following series of sentences might be used.

"How are you?"

"How old are you?"

"Who goes?"

"Who goes there?"

"Who goes there in the night?"

"One by one they took their places."

"One by one and two by two they took their places."

Speak each of these sentences on a single emission of breath. Having done these from a prone position, repeat sitting in a chair, then standing. Keep checking to make sure that you are breathing with your diaphragm.

Ninth, without changing techniques begin to work for more volume, gradually increasing loudness from phrase to phrase until you can be heard easily at the back of a large auditorium. Get the feeling of working harder with your diaphragm, not your throat. Projecting the voice requires energy, but if the energy is misplaced, it will harass the throat, cause a harsh quality, and place strain upon the vocal cords. You will not always need to use the amount of loudness you are now practicing. Voice, however, has the most power when it gives the impression of coming from an abundant reserve. Like driving a car with 300 horsepower, one does not need all the power at any one time. Knowledge of a generous reserve, however, gives the driver a secure feeling. It is therefore wise to practice projection from time to time.

After proper breathing habits have been fairly well established, the exercises should be continued a few minutes each day. This requires no extra time. They can be repeated while shaving, driving a car along a country road, or tending the furnace. It is advisable to read aloud a few minutes every day, watching breathing along with phrasing and pausing. As you read, after familiarizing yourself with the thought of the scripture or poem, you can concentrate on breathing.

What should be aimed at is the point when new breathing habits will carry over into formal speaking situations automatically. This may require some time. A man who has been breathing improperly many years should expect that it will require at least several months to break old habits and establish new ones.

The human voice is a marvelous, precise, and beautiful instrument. Any man can learn to use it with skillful effectiveness—but not without practice. Voice exercises of the kind we have just indicated can be profitable through one's whole life. A singer does not stop running the scale after he has left music conservatory; he practices some every day.

Practice need not be a time-consuming, boring task. After the first weeks needed to understand the techniques outlined in this chapter, they can be practiced daily with no inroads upon busy schedules. They can be performed in the midst of the daily routine. Relaxation can be practiced during a committee meeting; breathing, in the car on the way to and from the meeting!

We have been talking about foundations of effective voice. They should be understood only as *physical* foundations. There are other foundations, psychological in nature—foundations deeper still than any we have yet mentioned. In due time we shall have to come to grips with them, but meanwhile it should be remembered that speaking is partly a biological activity and that it can never rise above our mastery of the biological instruments which God has given us. As good stewards of our bodies, we should recognize the claims of good hygiene, including vocal hygiene.

5. *Ministerial Tune*

Ministerial tune is a hazard encountered by well-endowed speakers. It is a fault that grows out of many virtues. The name *ministerial* is unfortunate; for ministers are not the only ones using it. Some politicians are addicted; so are college professors. No public speaker may feel that he is forever secure from ministerial tune.

OFTEN UNRECOGNIZED BY ITS VICTIMS

A man may have a ministerial tune without realizing it. This, in fact, is part of the difficulty. A speaker with years of experience who can spot a tune in a fellow minister instantaneously may fail to detect it in himself. Even more perversely, he may be rather proud of the qualities of voice delivery which contribute to it. We remember a young minister with a musical bass voice who sang us to sleep every Sunday. He never learned what he was doing. The congregation contained a number of rapturous elderly ladies who fluttered around him at the end of each sermon and congratulated him on his wonderful pulpit voice. He drank in the praise and with each compliment sank deeper into the mire. How could he know that the only thing any of us were hearing was his voice? That his message never broke the sound barrier? There he stood, a man with a sermon behind a polished wall of sound; and there we sat before that shining surface. He could not get through

49

to us and we could not get through to him. All we could do was stare at the wall and wait for the end.

Since we began by saying that ministerial tune is a fault which comes from distorting several virtues of oral communication, perhaps we should indicate what some of those virtues are. One is a well-projected tone which can be heard clearly on the back row; adequate loudness is a *sine qua non* of good speaking, but since it is a departure from ordinary conversational practice it can easily lead to deviations from a conversational delivery. Another virtue is distinct articulation, which is essential to being understood. A speaker who is articulating clearly will round out the vowels and pronounce all the consonants and syllables; he will separate his words so that they can be caught as words rather than a jumble. This, too, may get out of hand. The consonants are over-articulated, and the vowels are unnecessarily prolonged, especially in words like *Lord* and *God*. The general impression is one of affectation, of sound for the sake of sound—an ingredient of the ministerial tune. Finally, the victim of a ministerial tune is a person who *cares* about his speeches; he has a strong emotional attachment to the ideas he is presenting, and he is deeply moved by the experience of sharing them with an audience. But such emotion may become a sea of feeling submerging and drowning the ideas.

Yes, if a man has these qualities of a good speaker—adequate loudness, clear articulation, and deep feeling—he may also have a ministerial tune. Few men have such a tune in ordinary conversation, though some do. This type of voice was satirized a few years ago in a radio series through the character of Digby Odell, "the friendly undertaker." Some speakers shift into the tune every time they speak in public; many, perhaps the majority, drift into it only in the longer, more sustained addresses and sermons which give full play to their feelings. So the native habitat of the ministerial tune for most ministers is the Sunday morning sermon.

Even so, how are you to know whether you have it? Go back to our earlier statement: A man can usually detect ministerial tune in another speaker, though he may not be aware that he himself is guilty of it. Here is the clue. Rely upon your assistant listener, or members of your class or workshop. With their help you will be able to listen to the tape recordings of your sermons, and if you have ministerial tune you will soon be able to detect it.

THE ANATOMY OF THE TUNE

A good method to use in listening to a tape for ministerial tune —once other listeners have indicated that they hear it—is to stop the tape at the end of each phrase for a number of phrases. Focus your attention upon the voice variables listed on the rating sheet under "Rate," "Pitch," and "Quality."

Rate.

All good speech has a rhythm, i.e., rate, but the rhythm of the ministerial tune is different. It is regular, almost hypnotic. In an intense conversation, which is the norm of speaking tempo, the rate is constantly shifting. But in ministerial tune there is little flexibility. The words dance in single file at about the same steady pace, phrase after phrase; each phrase has a beat, much like that of its predecessor and its successor. Isolating the beat from the words and meanings, it is even possible to plot the time pattern of such speaking. It may be five short beats followed by two or three long ones, or some other pattern equally rigid. The effect is not unlike that of a chant.

"Why do we do this?" you may be asking. We do not know exactly, but it seems not unlikely that it has something to do with the biological rhythms which nature has placed in every living being, both plant and animal. There is something in us, deeper than intellect, which makes us respond spontaneously to dance music and to the beat of a drum. And we do have a number of physical rhythms in us all the time—the heartbeat, the inhaling and exhaling of breathing, the electrical impulses over nerves from the brain, and many more. Mothers of young children have noticed that infants, barely able to walk, will stomp up and down in a kind of primitive dance; and that children even younger, when sitting up, will sometimes sway back and forth to a silent tempo.

It is not unreasonable to suppose that thought itself is pyramided upon these biological rhythms and that thinking may have its own rhythms. But the rhythms of thought, it would seem, are much more flexible—like those of a symphony. The rhythm of ministerial tune, by way of contrast, betrays an absence of thought; it is more like a chant.

We may say, then, that when thought abdicates the podium, the body will take over and direct the orchestra. And the only music it will call for, ignoring the wood winds, the harps, the violins, will be the drums. You may feel like entering a protest: "Do you mean to tell me that a man can deliver a speech without thinking about what he is saying?" That is precisely what we are saying. We do not say that he will not be thinking about his words, remembering them as if by rote or manufacturing them in a mechanical way; but we do say that he is not thinking his ideas spontaneously, individually, and concretely. If he were, they would come out in the varied rhythms of thought, not in the narrow rhythms of the body.

Intonation—Melody.

Ministerial tune combines a time pattern with a pitch pattern. All speech, of course, has melody. The pitch pattern of ministerial tune, however, like its rhythms, is narrow and limited. Like the endless repeating of one bar of a musical composition, it is monotonously repetitive. In other words, a speaker with ministerial tune uses his pitch changes in a stereotyped manner. Is this the primeval rhythm of the body breaking through again? It would seem so.

Inflection.

But there is more to this than biological rhythms. It has something to do with the emotions. Listen especially to the final inflections of the phrases, and you will begin to hear a consistent pattern here also. It is as if a generalized mood overrides individual feelings. This final inflection is frequently drawn out and sustained; and it often rises inconclusively. Listen to a recording of a sermon having this characteristic and ask, "What does this man feel? What is he saying emotionally?" You will have difficulty in answering your question, of course, but after a little reflection you may come up with something like this:

I think he's saying, "This is an important occasion. I want to succeed at it. I want you to be impressed with this sermon. And, moreover, I want you to feel, and I want to make myself feel, that this is a solemn occasion, not to be taken lightly or irreverently." You will probably sense that there is a general atmosphere of sadness. These emotions betray themselves in part through the inflections.

Quality.

We have already seen that resonation may vary a good deal and that changing quality is fundamentally dependent upon the changing muscle tensions in the larynx, throat, and mouth. In intense conversation, these tensions will keep varying to reflect a great variety of emotional states—pleasure, annoyance, excitement, boredom, pity, anger, fear, compassion. The use of resonation to convey feeling may be called *tone color*. Normally, like rate and pitch, it keeps changing to suit particular meanings; but in the stereotyped speech of the ministerial tune it stagnates or tends to stagnate on one emotion. This is frequently the emotion of sadness—a funereal quality invades and pervades the whole. It could be some other emotion—pugnacity, for example; but the thing that distinguishes it as ministerial is that it is sustained to override the particular emotional meanings which should be expressed.

Thus, if churchgoers were not so habitually overawed by the solemnity of their surroundings and so anesthetized by convention, they would often laugh outright at the ludicrous incongruity of thought and feeling in their minister's sermons. For example, suppose a man is saying, "Rejoice, and again I say rejoice! One of the unmistakable marks of genuine Christian character is joy. A Christian is deeply, infectiously happy!" One can say that so as to reflect the real joy which the words are meant to convey, or he can say it under the spell of a ministerial mood—as a kind of pulpit Digby Odell—and he will sound like a man on the verge of weeping. This means that intellectually, through words, he is saying one thing but emotionally, through tone color and inflection, he is saying exactly the opposite.

When the intellectual and the emotional modes are pulling in opposite directions, which are the people to believe? There is really no choice, for emotions are always stronger than ideas; and if we compel our listeners to choose between our ideas and our feelings about those ideas, they will instinctively believe our feelings and discount the ideas. If a minister is talking about the idea of joy, he must convey the feeling of joy at the same time; the intellectual and emotional modes must support one another. Otherwise the reaction of any serious listener, though not verbalized, may be like that of the Vermont farmer: "He talks considerable as I do when I'm lyin'."

HOW WE GOT THIS WAY

We do not mean to suggest by this last remark that ministers are hypocrites. We are saying that they sometimes sound that way. The matter is not shallow, nor is it simple. There are understandable reasons for it. Let us look at a few of them:

1. One reason ministers speak with a ministerial tune is that they think it is expected of them. Few men ever sat down and put it in so many words, but they drank in the idea through their pores from the surrounding atmosphere. One minister, who gave up a business career after he was forty to attend seminary, put it directly and simply: "When I started preaching I thought I needed a ministerial tune, so I acquired one." Few of us are as deliberate or self-conscious about it, but our reasons are the same: We speak with a tune because we think it is expected.

Churchgoers have heard preachers talk this way so long that they have come to identify preaching with a ministerial tune. The director of field work in the seminary from which we are writing often feels the pressure of this viewpoint. He sends out seminary men to candidate for rural pulpits only to have them rejected, in some cases, because "They don't preach. They just talk." What some churches seem to like is a man who can talk loud and fluently in the accepted ministerial manner. Whether he can think, whether he has commanding ideas to present, seem to be secondary or nonessential. Perhaps that is the reason some of these same churches seem so nearly dead. They are well insulated against ideas, and they do not choose to be disturbed if they can prevent it.

We shall have to admit, too, that there are probably some people who enjoy a well-cadenced ministerial tune. It makes no intellectual demands upon them. They can just lean back and be washed by a sea of words and bathed in a flood of pathos; they go away feeling vicariously purged. Of course, they have paid no real penance, only a sentimental penance; but that is what makes it all the more appealing. It is so satisfying, and it costs so little. Moreover, the insistent rhythms of a hypnotic voice speak to the primitive rhythms in people and they "go for it" the same way other people go for a jazz band.

What a minister will do about all this depends on whether he is trying to influence people or gain their superficial approval. If it is approval he wants, perhaps he had better fit the stereotype and let it go at that. But if he really wants to change people's minds, he had better learn how to talk with them man to man. It is like the difference between a politician and a statesman. Did you ever notice that campaigning politicians tend to speak in a ministerial tune? But real statesmen seldom have it.

Yes, a minister may speak with a tune because he thinks it is expected. It is a kind of audible union card showing that he belongs to the trade. He would never say it in such a bald, unflattering way, but that is what it amounts to. There are other reasons which may be operating.

2. A preacher may forget to locate the sermon where it really is to be found. He may locate it on paper in the outline, and especially in a neatly typed manuscript. There, in ordered sentences, he has said exactly what he meant. If he can learn it well and deliver it just as he has written it, he thinks, he will have a good sermon.

But he has made a serious mistake. The sermon is not on the paper. It is not even in the preacher. It is a spark that jumps from the preacher to the people in the living moment of delivery. It is conversation. It depends not only on preparation but also on communication. It requires of the preacher not only a vivid awareness of what he wants to say but an even more burning knowledge of why he needs to say it, and a creative concern for and empathic connection with the people with whom he speaks.

Instead of this living force which flows between himself and his people, his sermon becomes too individualistic. It is a solo performance. The people are needed, to be sure, but only as audience. They are not really integral to the sermon. And so it comes about that this particular sermon succeeds only for the preacher, in the study, but it is no sermon at all where it is needed.

We can never know how other people will behave. And to trust ourselves to this changing sea of human emotions requires a sailor's courage. Yet that is precisely what we have to do. Even the most polished sermon manuscript is not a sermon; it is only preparation. It can never be more than that. The sermon itself is the creative interchange of thought from the minister to the people and back.

Thus, no matter what preparation a man may have made in the study, he comes into the pulpit with an unfinished sermon. He must keep it so—unfinished and still living—or it will subside into generalized emotion or fall altogether into ministerial tune.

3. Again, a man may try to make his sermon a work of art. Preaching, it is true, belongs more to the arts than to the sciences, but its end product is not a beautiful sermon to be hung in the art gallery of the mind and admired for its technique. More especially it is not designed to bring honor and celebrity to the artist.

The secret motivations of a preacher can stray over into this mode of thinking so easily. Why does he preach? "To be seen of men" and praised by them. When he comes from the pulpit, he hungers for the approving word. He may even imagine himself eavesdropping on conversations of his churchgoers: "Wasn't that sermon marvelous this morning?" "Yes, I think we have the most wonderful minister. I don't think any preacher in town can hold a candle to him."

Of course, no minister would utter these daydreams aloud, or even admit them to himself; but the fact remains that a preacher can become a self-conscious artist displaying his masterpiece and waiting for the applause. And even if he does not want the applause, but only the finished masterpiece (art for art's sake), the end will be the same: ministerial tune.

The cure at this point is to discover the sermon as *help* for people in need. If an analogy must be found, a sermon is closer to the tool shed than to the art gallery.

4. Yet again, a man may fail to keep his sermon alive. It may have lived for him in the study until he wrote the last word of his manuscript—on Friday or Saturday. But time elapsed and he did nothing to make sure that the sermon was living on Sunday.

Actually, there are two phases to every true sermon—creation and resurrection. It has first to be created in the study; then it has to be raised from the dead on the first day of the week. This means that a preacher must take time to live his way back into that sermon on Sunday morning. We do not mean to master its outline and phrases merely, but to live himself into it—into its object and passion and into the moving reality of its truth.

This may take as much as two hours, but it is a kind of preparation that may not be by-passed. The object is to take a finished sermon and make it again an incomplete, growing thing for the unpredictable moment of delivery. Specific techniques for this must wait until later chapters, but the resurrection is essential. Otherwise, what a man has to say on Sunday morning will not be a sermon at all but only an obituary pronounced over a once-living idea.

Jesus apparently thought of preaching as sowing seed. He could not tell at the time of the sowing how much of it would take root and how much would be lost; but he went ahead with the sowing in faith, for the word was living, there was fertile soil in the lives of people, and the harvest could be plenteous.

A sermon at the time of its preaching is like the grain that sinks into the earth and dies that the plant of Christian insight and of Christian living may spring up and bring forth abundantly. How long will it be to the harvest? Growing seasons differ in different lives, and the growing time for some ideas is slower than for others. It may be a day or a year, or a quarter of a century. But no sermon lives in and of itself; it lives only in the harvest.

SOME PRACTICAL HELPS

From what we have already said, the directions for deliverance from ministerial tune already begin to emerge. And now, just to nail it all down in terms of a workable program for your use, we suggest, a few practical steps:

1. Prepare your sermons for people, not about subjects. You will, of course, present subjects and ideas, but you should present them to meet human needs—needs that are definitely felt and experienced in concrete terms. Phillips Brooks had things in right focus when he said in his famous Yale lectures on preaching: "Preach doctrine, preach all the doctrine that you know, and learn forever more and more; but preach it always, not that men may believe it, but that they may be saved by believing it." There is a vast difference between a subject-centered and a person-centered pulpit. Make yours person-centered.

2. Get your sermon in hand and be ready to rethink it with the congregation. Avoid memorizing it or reading it. Whatever paper you use, if you use any, use it only to prompt you in your conversation with the congregation.

3. Begin matter-of-factly. Try as much as possible to resist a stained-glass mentality. Even though you are in a pulpit, in church, on Sunday, try to talk with people in a natural, everyday manner—as you would talk in conversation about something that excites you.

4. Do not be afraid of emotion, but never try to emotionalize your speaking just for the sake of emotion itself. The emotion that is proper to a sermon cannot be imported into it; it must grow out of the ideas themselves, and it must be fitting to the ideas. The right feelings will appear naturally if they are deeply felt as they are shared. In other words, if you are on fire with an idea, and if you are sufficiently specific about it, the right emotion will come naturally from its source in your mind. But if you try to emotionalize your ideas you will get nothing but ministerial tune. Remember,

too, that emotion which draws attention to itself is not genuine emotion at all; it is only sentimentality. Feeling, as we shall see in the next chapter, is primarily a by-product of seeing. Concentrate upon seeing into your subject deeply and concretely and then let the emotions rise; do not be afraid of them.

5. Speak to people as individuals. Do not bunch them together as a crowd or a mass. One of the worst bits of instruction ever given to public-school classes in speaking is the one that keeps coming to our attention through badly misled seminary students: "When you speak, do not look at the people, but fasten your eyes on the back wall, just above the people's heads." This is a piece of mischievous nonsense. When you talk with people look at them, one by one, and see what they are saying back to you pantomimically. Keep yourself in dialogue with your listeners. Some ministers address their small congregations as though they were vast concourses of two thousand people. The late Charles H. Spurgeon is said to have addressed two thousand people as though he were speaking personally to one man.

6. Stop trying to be so impressive. Let your message make the impression. It is difficult, if not impossible, to give two impressions simultaneously—that Jesus Christ is mighty and that you are exceedingly clever. Locating importance where it truly belongs— with God, in the Gospel, and in people—you are free to worry less about the impression *you* are making. Increased naturalness will result. Ministerial tune will no longer exist.

6. *Speaking with Your Whole Body*

Although the audible aspects of communication (the voice variables) are of tremendous importance, the process of effective communication does not end with them. If it were possible for the average minister or public speaker to deliver his message over a public-address system from the privacy of his study, this chapter would not be necessary. We could continue to concentrate only on what is *heard*—the voice, the words, the ideas—and ignore entirely what is seen.

The average speaker today, however, can scarcely escape the fact that the occasions when he can speak to an audience without being seen are rare. Radio still exists, to be sure, but the success of television only serves to prove the point—audiences prefer not only to hear speakers but to see them.

We are well acquainted with pantomimes in which an abundance of meaning can be conveyed and entire plays performed without having a single word spoken. We have all personally experienced thousands of times the meanings transmitted to us by a smile or a frown, an extended hand or a head turned away, a brisk stride or a shuffle. Words are unnecessary as the inaudible thoughts are expressed visibly through posture, facial expressions, and physical activities. (It is interesting in this connection to note that despite our many different national languages the symbols of bodily expression seem to be universal.)

It follows then that whenever we go into a pulpit or onto a platform our bodies go along to play their own pantomimes, to tell their own stories whether we like it or not. And this is not at all undesirable except when our bodies speak one thing and our words the exact opposite. In such cases the effect on our listeners is usually one of neutral apathy as one message cancels out the other.

To be a convincing speaker, therefore a man must add to vocal or audible effectiveness physical or visual effectiveness. In short, he must learn to communicate with his whole body.

There are three possible relationships of a speaker's body to his delivery of a speech: (1) His body may go into the pulpit with him like a passive, inert passenger merely "going along for the ride." The performance of such a speaker is ghostlike. He speaks as if he were nothing but head; nothing below his neck has any share in what he is doing. If there were any way to arrange it, his body could just as well be absent, on a fishing expedition or playing golf.

There is a second possibility. (2) A speaker's body may accompany him like a mischievous boy bent upon distracting attention. There is bodily agitation, but it does not support or strengthen what is being said. Rather, it divides the attention of hearers, diverting or annoying them. To cast it into the language of the theater, such a speaker's mind is like a dramatic actor who has learned all his lines, but when he gets on stage his body, like a self-conscious "ham," keeps upstaging him. The things such a speaker's body may do are numerous, varied, and often ludicrous. One man taps his right foot like a nervous musician; the rhythmic thump-thump-thump is audible throughout the church or hall. Another teeters nervously from heel to toe and keeps bouncing up and down. Still another man removes his glasses and plays with them. We have heard of one preacher, back in the days of the frock coat, who reached down to the hem of his garment and rolled it up in his right hand until he came to the lapel; then he let it fall and started all over again. The young people were fascinated. Their chief concern each Sunday was to keep tally, to see how many times he completed the stunt. Some flail the air with windmill arms. Others prance like caged animals. The body is in the pulpit, but it is distracting from the sermon.

Pulpit clowning and platform calisthenics of these and other varieties may account in no small measure for the starchiness of much modern delivery. Extremes react to create their opposite. But the cure for bad action is not inaction.

We need to grasp the secret of the third alternative: (3) A speaker's body may bring to his speech the whole weight and total force of personality. Words are then more than words; they are also things.[1] And a sermon, for example, is not only a talk about religion; it is a live demonstration of it. When a preacher learns to speak with his whole body, his sermon will be like a printed musical score which is transformed into audible music by a well-conducted symphony orchestra.

We are, of course, talking about gesture; but until now we have not used the word because its meaning has been too narrowly restricted. It has usually been identified with an elocutionary use of the hands, a pompous manual posturing. Hand motions are included in true gesturing, of course, but they form only a small fraction of your real gestures. Your hands are expressive in the best sense only when your whole body is expressive along with them. And even then, they are expressive not because you manipulate them properly but because they are instruments of your thoughts just as your words are. They come from within. Gestures include lifting your eyebrows, shrugging your shoulders, stooping, or standing erect. Clenching your fist, pointing a finger, smiling, frowning, and lifting your foot—all these are gestures. But all of them should live from within.

By now it is quite obvious that a mechanical approach to gestures will produce nothing better than a kind of pulpit or platform puppetry. The key to living gesture is found not in a special set of directions but in the natural reactions of daily conversation.

[1] Interesting biblical insight into the concrete unity of speech and action is found in the fact that the Hebrew word dābhār means both word and thing.

Let us illustrate. Suppose we ask you a question. "What is the price of a Lincoln automobile?" If you are an average preacher, your reply will probably be, "How should I know? Preachers don't have that kind of money!" These were your words but you said much more than can be read in the words alone. You raised your eyebrows; you wrinkled your forehead; you shrugged your shoulders, and lifted your hands from your elbows, palms upward. And you did all this as you were saying the words.

When we point this out, you say, "Did I really do all that? I wasn't aware that I was doing anything." Of course you were unaware of your gestures, but you had an idea which you *felt* and you expressed it simultaneously through words and through gestures, or pantomime. When an idea is vividly and spontaneously thought, it expresses itself quite normally in physical action and also in audible speech, both at the same time; and both the words and the actions manage to be a unified expression of the same idea.

Try an experiment. Watch conversing people at a distance sometime, just out of earshot. Notice how they talk with their whole bodies—facial expression, hands, arms, and posture. Ordinarily we listen to what people say without being aware that we also watch them for clues to the full meaning of what they are saying. Merely separate your listening from your watching for a few moments and you will begin to realize that people normally speak with their whole bodies. In fact, most people gesture eloquently.

But take these same people into a pulpit or onto a platform, and what happens? Either they are frozen into defensive inaction or they are prodded into unnatural poses and grotesque mannerisms. They become wooden Indians or cats on a hot tin roof. (For clarity's sake we overstate the case.) Something very like this happens—or tends to happen—to all public speakers, including preachers. One reaction—that of the wooden Indian—is inhibition, a kind of self-conscious self-control which is really an expression of fear or anxiety. The other reaction—the cat on the hot tin roof—is just as self-conscious but not so well controlled. In either reaction, mind and body are divided against each other and convey opposing impressions. They expose a speaker who is unable to lose his painful self-consciousness in the concrete realities of his message and in living interaction with his hearers.

Apply these insights to pulpit speaking, probe for causes, and you will probably come up with two: on the one hand the inhibition of physical action; on the other hand, a failure of creativity. Let us examine these in turn.

INHIBITION

The man whose body seems inert in the pulpit may be using up a tremendous amount of physical and nervous energy to inhibit his natural actions. He may be holding himself rigid. To the listeners it seems that he is only partially in his sermon; and this impression is not misleading for he is actually withholding himself from it. He does not want to make a full commitment lest he make a fool of himself and appear ridiculous. So he is defensive, "on guard."

Probably it never occurs to him that his very defensiveness is a physical action in itself, and that it has its own message. You can illustrate this for yourself. Stand erect and tense your muscles as though you were waiting for someone to spring through the door to attack you with a club. Your actions are inhibited in anticipation of the action you will take when the danger takes definite shape. But suppose the danger lingers, that it does not put forth its head, but that you continue waiting for it. This is much the situation of a "starchy," inhibited speaker. He is on guard, defensive, controlling himself, preparing to ward off an attack. And he is saying all of these things about his anxious state of mind in pantomime. So even the inhibited speaker is talking with his body; but the message of his body vetoes the message of his lips. His lips say, "Fear not and be of good courage," but his bodily inhibition says, "I myself am paralyzed by fear and I have little courage." His lips say, "Blessed are they who give good measure poured out of generous heart." But his rigid body says, "I know little about giving. Most of my energy is used in clutching what I have and in protecting myself."

The inhibited speaker has an immense problem. He will not

solve it until he understands himself better and learns to let go internally. We shall be saying more about this in the section on personality in Chapter 7, but while we are on this point, let us enter an observation that may seem somewhat marginal. We have noticed that some of the starchiest preachers we have heard are men who do a good deal of clowning in conversation and before small, informal groups. Sometimes closer acquaintance shows that the clown-face is a mask behind which there cowers a frightened little boy. The mask of the clown is not appropriate for the pulpit —so he seems to think—so when he ascends to this lofty station he puts on another mask and becomes "old sobersides." Both disguises are poor substitutes for the warmly human, needy person who lives beneath them.

FAILURE IN CREATIVITY

Inhibition may not be in the picture at all. The trouble may be a simple failure to speak living ideas which are alive for the speaker *at the moment of delivery*. In such a case gesture will be absent or inappropriate. This is not to say that the ideas were not once living, born and breathing in the study, but that now they are all corpses, dead and lifeless in the pulpit. And they come out as words, mere words, ghostly survivors of the flesh-and-blood beings that once lived and wrought righteousness. The sad fact is that many so-called sermons from the pulpit are not sermons at all but requiems.

Admittedly, we have given the preacher in question the benefit of the doubt. We have supposed that he is a committed Christian and that he did prepare his sermons well. If these were not the facts, there could be other reasons why creativity failed: (1) The ideas of the sermon may be second hand, expressions of what the preacher thinks he is supposed to believe, but no coin which he has dug out of the rock for himself and minted in his own shop. (2) He may have skimped the preparation of his sermon. It may have failed to live again because it never lived at all.

A committed, conscientious man who prepares carefully may also fail to be physically alive and fully creative in the pulpit. The possible reasons are many. (1) His memory fades. In the lapse of time from sermon preparation to sermon delivery the original message may have faded in the speaker's mind.

(2) His concentration fails. The preacher's attention may be distracted and divided as he speaks so that he is not rallying all his powers to the one end of delivering his sermons to his people. Other thoughts intrude: thoughts about the order of service, thoughts about room temperature and the duties of the ushers, thoughts about individuals before him, or duties of the morrow, or about the impression he is making. Again, he may be concentrating on his sermon, but his mind may be running ahead, giving more attention to what he is going to say in the next moment than to what he is saying now. Yet again, he may be so occupied with exact diction, phraseology, and other vocal niceties that he cannot attend fully to the ideas which the words are meant to convey. It all boils down to a simple fact: There are things in the speaker's mind which are in competition with each part of his sermon in the living moment of delivery.

(3) His imagination is inactive. To be alive, a sermon must rise out of the real world of objects, events, and persons; and it must throb with this world of color and sound, this onrushing, churning river of tastes and odors, of heat and chill, of surfaces memorized by sensitive fingertips and burdens felt on aching shoulders. In a word, a living sermon goes back to the grass roots of human experience—not to concepts, but to percepts; not to words but to things. This idea may be a little difficult to grasp at first, but it is crucial. Let us see if we can get to the root of it.

We sometimes suppose that thinking begins with words, but there is evidence that it begins deep down in the preverbal world. Introspect a bit, and perhaps you can formulate the thinking process in words. To introspective experience it seems that the words do not make the idea; they merely express it. It is, of course, very hard to catch ourselves in the act of thinking, for thinking is the arresting of a process, a stepping aside from activity to analyze the activity. So we can never be certain as to what exactly does go on even in that intimate inner world of our own minds. But we can try to see it, and somewhat dimly we do distinguish a few things.

We do not here propose a theory for the whole life of the mind. Shades of Plato with his doctrine of reminiscence and of Kant with his a priori categories warn us away from these rocky coasts! But about the *content* of consciousness, the material about which we think, we seem to be clear: There is nothing in the mind that was not first in the senses. The things that we think and talk about must go back to particular experiences; and the main channels through which these experiences come to us are the five senses. Sense experiences—sights, sounds, smells, tastes, and the feel of objects, as well as our own internal bodily feelings—are all stored away in memory. Then the memory, with all of these concrete sensual images in it, is drawn upon by imagination and by the organizing powers of the mind in ways we little understand and is finally put into words.

This means that thought starts in remembered or imagined sensual images. Only when words come out of this concrete sensual world in the imagination are they alive. Let us take an example. Suppose we say, "Universal education is a necessary basis for democracy." What happens as we formulate that thought? We do not begin with the word *education*. One of us will see the red country schoolhouse which he attended as a boy in jeans, or he may see the county seat high school; perhaps he will hear the school band playing, or the sound of his Latin teacher directing a recitation. In other words, he draws upon his own concrete experiences which for him add up to *education*. He does not take time to remember them all, of course, but he calls upon a few of them to stand for the general idea, to symbolize it, so to speak. These are prelogical symbols. They come before words.

To complete the idea about education as the basis of democracy we need a sensual symbol for *democracy*. One person may hear the strains of the "Star-Spangled Banner"; another may see a visual image of the national Capitol or the town hall of his boyhood village. There are thousands of possible symbols, but all of them can be seen, heard, tasted, or touched.

Now we need to *relate* these two ideas of education and democracy. One, we said, was the *foundation* of the other. We could do it this way: In imagination we see a vast horde of medieval serfs, somewhat like Edwin Markham's *Man With the Hoe*. We form them into a foundation for the Capitol building in Washington, D.C. It is too heavy for them—they are bent and weak in their ignorance. They cannot uphold it. It will crush them. In contrast, we imagine another foundation made of the living bodies of strong, upright college graduates. The Capitol does not rest upon their bent shoulders, but they triumphantly lift it up, strong and confident, upon their upthrust hands. Minds made free in the school are ready for the world of free elections; young people who have learned to think for themselves are ready to govern themselves!

Every person will formulate his idea differently and from a differing resource of perceptual images, but something like this takes place as we bring our ideas out of the formless mass of consciousness into the articulate shapes of language. Thinking starts in the imagination with the sensual images derived through memory from the five senses. So, when we think, we have a kind of chain reaction: sensual experiences—memory—imagination—organization—words.

When we connect all this to speaking in public, it is apparent that in preparing a speech we do have to forge the chain of thought out of the raw materials of the senses. But when we get into the pulpit, since we have already put our thoughts into words, we may just speak the words without re-creating them from the beginning. Speakers often do this. Their words are not real, living thoughts, but only the shadows of thoughts that once were living.

The only cure is to reactivate the imagination. Since the imagination of most people is perfectly healthy in conversation, all we need to do is to get speakers into the conversational frame of mind—not making a declamation, but talking with people about the things that matter, and doing it with a flexible body which unconsciously responds to the things perceived.

The response of the body to perceptions remembered or imagined is pantomime or gesture. It is the action of the whole body: facial muscles, legs, arms, torso, shoulders, neck, hands, face, and forehead. It is the one sure sign that a speaker is really reliving what he is talking about.

The sensual capacities of people seem to differ somewhat. One man may be predominantly *visual*; he *sees* his ideas before he puts them into words. Another is *audile*; he *hears* his ideas, like scraps of dialogue, snatches of music, or a bit of noise such as the sounds of city traffic. Still another person will *feel* his ideas as muscular or motor impulses. He has been called a *motile*. Most people, of course, have all five senses, and all five of them are active in perception and in memory and imagination. Moreover, the larger the number of stimuli that coalesce to make up an idea, and the more detailed and vivid they are, the more alive the idea is when it is finally spoken as a word. Actors, for example, have an extremely rich, varied and detailed perceptual imagination.

But suppose someone is strongly motile and very weak in other sensual perceptions? He should probably not be a speaker. There is a story about Pavlova, the celebrated dancer. Someone asked her to tell him what one of her dances meant, and she replied, "If I could have said it, do you think I would have danced it?" Some people do not express themselves in words primarily. Apparently motor feelings rise into the realm of words with greater difficulty than do visual and auditory sensations. Most of us need not worry, however, for we find our senses in fairly good balance. Our point of failure in most cases is not in native endowment but in careless use.

The main thing is for a speaker to make sure that there is a constant stream of concrete sensual images back of his words at all times. He can rehearse his speech with this in mind and make certain that the talking motion picture of his mind is operating—in technicolor, if possible.

At this point discouragement may enter. Creative delivery depends on the activity of the sensual imagination. But upon what does the sensual imagination depend? Is there anything to be done about it? Yes, there are two things that can be done. The first lies in immediate preparation; the second, in exercises to strengthen the imagination.

IMMEDIATE PREPARATION

Immediate preparation involves sensitizing oneself to the sensory stimuli lying back of the message. The whole process has been spelled out in great detail by R. W. Kirkpatrick in his helpful book, *The Creative Delivery of Sermons*.[2] In general, the process calls for reading or speaking the sermon aloud slowly, making sure that every phrase comes alive through sensory images. When words recall nothing but abstract ideas or point only to other words, they must be held before the mind until they begin to suggest concrete images. If this process fails, the phrases must be lowered down the ladder of abstraction until they come closer to the world of daily experience. An hour spent with a sermon, working on it in this fashion, will greatly increase the creativity of delivery.

STRENGTHENING THE IMAGINATION

Exercises to strengthen the imagination begin by making us more observant, more alert to what is going on in the world around us. This is done by submitting us to tests of what we see and hear in some typical situation. We go out and look in a store window, let us say, and come back to outline exactly what we have seen— giving as many details as possible. Again, such exercises depend upon strengthening the memory. We recount an experience, reliving it and acting it out in great detail—first at the place where it happened, then in a different setting. Finally, the exercises increase our power of imagination by getting us to identify ourselves with persons unlike ourselves as we act out things that happened to them and respond to certain events and objects. The truth of the matter is that we live in the midst of the wonders and glories of the world seeing and hearing only a little of it. Nature is a bush aflame with God, but only those who see take off their shoes. The rest of us pick blackberries. But we do not have to remain so dull of ear and eye. We can hear and see more. We can

[2] Macmillan, 1947.

remember more vividly. And we can learn to re-create for ourselves the experiences of others. Exercises to help with this will be found in Appendix C, pp. 148-152. They are well worth doing, for the secret of creative speaking lies in an active imagination.

There is one fairly obvious implication of all this. Illustrate your sermons well. The more specific and concrete they are, the easier it will be to re-create them.

There is another implication. Always talk about things that are real to you. The religion that can be communicated is the religion that has been experienced in actual, live encounters. Speculations and philosophizing are never adequate. We can do no better than to follow the example of the original preachers, one of whom wrote: "That which was from the beginning, which we have *heard*, which we have *seen with our eyes*, which we have looked upon and *touched with our hands* . . . we proclaim also to you." (I John 1:1-3.) This is a scripture which has application for every public speaker. A preacher should have it engraved on the back of the pulpit where he must read it every Sunday as he begins his sermon.

Although a special section on personality will appear presently, we cannot complete our discussion about posture, gesture, and physical action without touching briefly on personality. Gestures and muscle tensions are closely related, and tensions (as we have noted previously) have a lot to do with voice quality. Habitual posture also tells us a good deal about a man. If he stands tall with chest and head erect he exudes self-confidence; but if he hunches his shoulders and fastens his gaze on the floor he shows a very different basic attitude. If he enters the pulpit or mounts the platform with firm, confident stride he tells us something quite different from what he says when he minces along apologetically with every part of his physical being headlining the fact that he would rather hide than be seen.

Posture is fundamentally a matter of mental attitude. A speaker is at his best when his mind is elevated by an idea and when he is eager to share it with his listeners. He will, therefore, move with assurance to the place from which he will speak, and once in position he will stand tall, almost as though suspended from the ceiling by an invisible wire attached to his chest. This will balance him on the balls of his feet and he will be free to respond physically to anything he thinks or feels, and his bodily movements will be natural and graceful. If he is truly elevated by his ideas, and if he is ready and willing to give himself unreservedly to his hearers, he will not be tense, but free. When he extends his arms they will be fully extended, not partially protruded like the head of a turtle, fearfully exploring his surroundings. He will be no marionette operated by invisible strings but a living, active, confident person.

In other words, both posture and gesture have to come from the inside, from what we are thinking and feeling. And these come out as they should *if*: if a man is on fire with his message, if his ideas are real to him one by one as he delivers them, if his perceptual imagination is active, if he trusts and likes people he is talking to, and if he likes himself and feels personally secure. Wrong posture and poor gestures can be recognized externally, but they must be corrected from the inside, and they come best from a completely integrated, undefensive personality.

An effective speaker has taken off the armor and torn down the fortresses around himself. He is open and free with his hearers. And he shares his life and thoughts with them through his whole being.

7. *What Are You Saying Emotionally?*

A speech or sermon is much more than audible words. In the previous chapter we saw that it is the communication of a whole person —body as well as mind, sensual percepts as well as mental concepts. To put it another way, every time a person stands up to speak he communicates in two languages simultaneously. One is the language of the mind—the intellectual mode. The other is the language of the feelings—the emotional mode. These two simultaneous communications need not say the same thing. In fact, they may and often do say exactly opposite things, in which case the message of the words (the intellectual mode) is not merely diminished by the contrary message of the feelings (the emotional mode); it is actually canceled. The principle at work in such a vetoing of words is very simple: *When the intellectual and emotional modes are at variance with each other, people instinctively choose the emotional message and disregard the intellectual.* This fact makes it vitally important for a speaker to know what he is saying through the emotional mode, and imperative for him to bring his emotions into full support of his ideas.

EMOTIONAL SENSITIVITY

Do people really hear our emotions? On the surface it seems such a sophisticated and discriminatory kind of listening that only highly trained psychologists could be capable of it. In actual fact, children are more sensitive to it than most adults, and uneducated people than most men with Ph.D. degrees. This is not strange, for an infant has feelings before he has ideas and he learns to express many of them quite eloquently—a gurgle of contentment, a squall of anger, a shriek of fear. The language of emotions is our first and our deepest communication. Why, then, should we have difficulty in hearing it?

We do hear it. Immediately and clearly. When we hear emotion, of course, we do not ordinarily respond with our understanding; rather we respond with feelings. And we do all of this without being aware that we are doing it. Thus, a speech can be a complete success intellectually but remain a total failure because the hearers reject it unconsciously on the basis of negative feelings. On the other hand, they may like it immensely because the speaker gives emotional support to his ideas and establishes emotional rapport with his hearers. It is then that a speech is truly *moving*, and only then. Yes, we do hear a speaker's feelings.

Not only do listeners receive the emotional message of a speech but they can usually put that emotional communication into words. Students called upon to do this sometimes fumble for words as they articulate such feelings, it is true, but this is not because it is difficult to *sense* the emotion. The only difficulty comes in bringing the awareness of the emotion from the margins into the focus of attention and in finding appropriate words for it.

After members of a class have heard a sermon or other speech, they can usually unearth the emotional message by asking three questions:

How does the speaker feel toward his message?
What does he feel toward himself?
What are his feelings toward his audience?

Experience has shown that answers to these questions are always forthcoming, that they are usually rather precise, and that the speaker himself finds the judgment valid. It has also been discovered that the speaker himself, when he listens to a tape recording of his speech in company with an alert and sympathetic listener, is usually able to answer these questions about his own speech.

This is a searching, probing thing to do to a speech and its maker, and it should be done only within the context of genuine concern and fellow feeling from one or more trusted friends. It should always be done from the desire to help, never from a desire to hurt. There is a rule of thumb which may prove useful: *If you find yourself taking pleasure in criticizing your "friend," you are secretly wounding him for your own gratification; but if you find it difficult to criticize him, if you feel compelled to do it in his interest but against your own inclinations, you are probably helping him.* You cannot knock a man down as long as you have your arm around him. We need to realize that such probing into the emotions of a speaker may create a personal crisis for him; and we should not be willing to plunge him into it unless we are willing to see him through it.

A FEW CASES

Let us look at a few typical profiles of emotion as revealed by sermons from a course in practice preaching. The feelings of the preachers were put into words by their fellow students:

Case A. "He has a good sermon and he is proud of it. In fact, he almost defies anyone to criticize it. His ideas are clear and logical, but he uses them as a club. He expects to overpower us, to convince us even if he has to convince us against our wills. I'd say he was authoritarian, that he trusts himself, but that he does not trust us. He's trying to force something down our throats. He has a fervent belief in his 'truth,' and great faith in himself, but he has no love for us."

Case B. "He is very much on the defensive. He throws out a statement in a tentative manner and waits to see how we are going to react to it; then he tosses out another. It's a kind of cat-and-mouse operation, as though he were the mouse and we are all cats. He wants to make friends with us but he's afraid we will eat him. He's not certain of his ideas, and he seems to be divided within himself. He doesn't dislike us. He's just afraid of us."

Case C. "He likes us all immensely. He is warm and accepting toward us. He thinks people are fun, and we have a good, clean feeling after we have listened to him. But he doesn't seem to get inside his sermon; I can never remember anything in particular that he talked about. His words seem to move faster than his ideas; he doesn't feel them at the time he's speaking them. There's just a general atmosphere of sincerity and earnestness—and I can get that without half thinking, so I just drowse through his sermon. He didn't make me listen, but as a person I like him and I'd trust him with anything."

Case D. "He talks like a man in a dream. Things just aren't real. They are fairyland make-believe. He seems friendly enough and sincere enough but he's up in the clouds being a visionary. When he walked up into that pulpit he left the real world and ascended into a lofty realm which he would like to possess but which is not his now. He doesn't look like himself or sound like himself. He seems to think that his ordinary, everyday life isn't good enough for the pulpit. I wonder if he's imitating somebody. And, oh, isn't it all so sad?"

THE PREACHER'S REACTION

The reaction of any preacher to such a candid and searching report from one or more of his friends will be almost traumatic. He may be seized with panic. He may feel like a frightened animal in a cage; and he will want to know what he can do to burst out of his prison. How can he learn to speak truly in the emotional mode, to undergird his intellectual message with deep and authentic feelings?

There is no easy answer, but there is an answer. It is not easy, because emotions cannot be produced directly or manipulated at will. Emotions can be simulated, of course; but when they are thus manufactured to order, their bogus quality is apparent and they call attention to themselves. This is not true emotion, but mere emotionalism. One might call it sentimentalism, which has been defined as emotion experienced for its own sake. There is no room in good preaching for emotionalism or sentimentalism. True emotion does not call direct attention to itself; rather, because it is appropriate to each idea as it is being expressed, it calls attention to the idea and powerfully reinforces that idea.

Genuine emotion is the result of seeing an idea clearly and concretely and of assenting to it with one's whole being. As long as ideas are general and abstract, they glance off our minds; when they become specific they penetrate, and they draw blood.

We are directed to think of not one but two levels of emotion in a given speech or sermon. There are, on the one hand, a man's profoundest feelings, his real attitudes toward his fellows and toward himself. These attitudes persist day by day, from speech to speech, and permeate all other activities. They are imbedded in a man's character; they become matters of personality. This emotional factor in speaking is sometimes called *pathos*. It is feeling's deepest level. On the other hand, there are a man's immediate feelings about a given speech or sermon. There is the way he feels about this particular speech. He likes some speeches more than others. Some have refused to develop as he wanted them to, but he must deliver them although he cannot wax very enthusiastic about them. There is also the way he feels about the situation in which he is speaking: Is he glad to be here, with these people, on this occasion? Does he feel at ease? Does he really want to share something with his hearers? And is his message vividly *real* and *alive* for him—sensually alive, concretely and specifically experienced? All these questions relate to immediate attitudes which may change from speech to speech. This particular emotional factor in speaking, to be distinguished from *pathos*, has been called *melism*.

We can do something directly about melism. Improvement at this point will be the result of industry and application. The first requirement is more prolonged and more intensive preparation of each sermon. We have to live with an idea until it possesses us, until we are on fire with it. This takes time and study. The second requirement is real pastoral acquaintance with the needs of people and a sincere desire to help people. This will require unceasing pastoral work.

But time, study, and pastoral care are not enough by themselves. We also have to develop perceptual imagination. Since this was discussed in the previous chapter and there are also exercises for this purpose in Appendix C, we will not dwell upon it here. However, it may be said that a speaker with a sluggish perceptual imagination will be seriously defective in melism and will find no remedy for his trouble short of developing a more acute ear and a sharper eye as the basis of a clearer memory and a more agile imagination. There are ways of attaining this. (See pp. 148-152.)

PERSONALITY

While something can be done immediately and directly about *melism, pathos* involves lifelong attitudes having roots back in the hidden years of childhood. Most of these attitudes are unconscious. Until friends point them out, or they are recognized from the tape recording, a speaker seldom realizes he has them. He may even have supposed that his deepest feelings were quite opposite to what they really are. This is not at all unusual. People often hide their motives and feelings from themselves, and preachers are no exception.

Now we come to the hard fact: Undesirable personality traits cannot be changed by an act of will. Instead, we have to achieve self-insight and self-acceptance. To put it in religious language, we have to die to the old self and be reborn as a new creation. There may be other contexts within which this can be accomplished but the only one known to the authors is that of two or more persons, i.e., the context of personal counseling. While the label is relatively new and we have been made very much aware of it by modern psychology, the method itself is very old. It is found in the Roman Catholic confessional when the confessional is at its best, and it is also found in what Protestants have called "the priesthood of all believers" when that doctrine is rightly applied. Under the name of "pastoral counseling" few modern ministers remain unacquainted with this movement. Moreover, thousands of us have witnessed the therapeutic powers of counseling as we ourselves have seen it from the role of the counselor.

Writers like Seward Hiltner and Carrol Wise[1] have given us the handles to this important skill. And many of us have used these skills—upon others. But we ourselves have not submitted to counseling. We have felt, perhaps, that we could work out our own personal problems by introspection or by private prayer. What we are secretly hoping in this kind of reasoning is that we can meet and overcome our personal problems without undergoing the humiliation that laying them all out before human eyes involves. The humiliation of a perfectly candid counseling situation *is* a kind of dying, and we would rather escape it at almost any cost; but the truth is, there can be no radical change in character without it. To be born again, one has first to die. To become a new person, a man has first to receive a wound where it hurts him the most—in his pride. Until something like this happens all his prayers to God are pretense. He is saying, "God, change me, but don't let it cost me anything."

The time may be fast approaching when every man entering the ministry will undergo personal counseling as a regular part of his seminary course. Until a man comes to understand himself he is ill equipped to know his fellows. Or his God.

There is no space here to discuss what is so fully treated in the literature on the subject, except to survey briefly some of the leading factors involved in achieving mental health.

1. A sense of need is essential. Need may be discovered by asking an objective friend to comment on the personality traits we reveal during a sermon. If our friend hears us expressing feelings of fear or hostility we should be sufficiently alarmed to take action.

2. A counselor whom one likes, trusts, and respects is necessary. This man need not be trained. His principal requirements are to be able to listen intelligently enough to develop real empathy and

[1] Seward Hiltner, *Pastoral Counseling* (Abingdon, 1949). Carrol Wise, *Pastoral Counseling: Its Theory and Practice* (Harper, 1951).

to accept without moralizing whatever feelings, attitudes, or experiences are verbalized.

3. Evaluation is required to analyze the nature of the problem. This means reviewing past and present experiences, attitudes, and feelings in concrete detail and telling the counselor all about them, particularly those one would like most to conceal.

4. Insight must be achieved. When a person begins to see *why* he has felt as he has he is not far from insight. Insight will come as something that is given, if there is complete honesty in sharing.

5. Catharsis is experienced. When insight comes it will bring a great sense of release, and it will be followed by a new capacity to accept oneself and to like other people.

MINISTERIAL PITFALL

Before we go farther, it should be noted that ministers live under pressures which make self-understanding and self-acceptance especially urgent. It is easy for the man who preaches a lofty ideal to find himself under the condemnation of that ideal because it remains unattained in his own life. The ministry is a lofty calling demanding a man's best, so most ministers set a high ideal for themselves and keep trying to achieve it. But no man, from the nature of the ideal, ever quite succeeds in measuring up to it. As long as he knows he is not succeeding, and as long as he accepts his own imperfections, he is safe; but this is not as easy as it sounds.

There are many subtle pressures at work here. A man preaches about his ideal; he gets to imagining that he has attained it, because he talks about it so much. Other people expect a minister to be good enough to be a minister. He doubles his will power and drives on toward his ideal with gritted teeth. Very gradually and very subtly he becomes a misguided Pharisee, trying to earn acceptance before God and men by his own good deeds.

This puts a wall between a minister and his people. It throws him on the defensive. When such a man climbs the pulpit stairs he is climbing up to his ministerial ideal. So, when he is in his pulpit he is not plain John Brown; he is Moses on Sinai or Paul on Mars' Hill.

No man is good enough for the Christian ministry; that is a part of the paradox of the calling. No man is perfect, and a minister is no different from anybody else. But, like anybody else, a minister does not have to rely on his own merit and his own goodness. He does not need to be the dynamo that generates all his moral power. He can hook up to the big dynamo. He is somewhat like an alcoholic who has become sober through Alcoholics Anonymous; he can help others, not because he is without fault or above blame, but because he has found a power not himself that makes for sobriety or righteousness. If we could be fully good all by ourselves we would not need God or our fellows; we would be our own gods.

Do not misunderstand. Preaching relies upon personal power. A Christian preacher must be a good man, but he must be good in the Christian sense, not in the Pharasaic sense. John Knox in *The Integrity of Preaching* puts the matter clearly:

And let there be no misunderstanding about what I mean by "how good we are." I mean how honest we are, how straightforward and sincere, how free from pride, sham, pretentiousness, self-complacency, of preoccupation with our own problems. I mean how penitent we are, with what passion of desire we are seeking God, how ready we are to submit to his will, how concerned we are to please him, how constantly aware we are of our need of his forgiveness, how faithfully dependent upon his grace, how unyielding in our discipline, how unwithholding in our devotions. I mean how genuinely concerned we are about others, how eager to understand and help them, how patient with them and how loving, and how sensitive to their deeper wants because we are living truly and deeply ourselves.[2]

A preacher who is a good man in terms of Knox's picture cannot fail to exert a tremendous power for Christian goodness through his spoken message. At this stage of human knowledge we do not understand much about the way human personality discloses itself in human speech, but we do know that it comes through. One of the authors had occasion recently to talk with a university senior who has been blind for the past four years—a young man singu-

[2] Abingdon, 1957, pp. 59, 60.

larly without self-pity and singularly open to his world. We asked him if he formed any conclusions about the character of people from their voices. "Oh, yes," he said. "A man's voice is the most revealing thing about him. It is pretty hard for him to hide behind it."

When we come to this aspect of preaching, there is no way of preparing the sermon without preparing the man. No one has said this better than the late great Phillips Brooks of Boston:

Preaching is the communication of truth by man to men. It has in it two essential elements, truth and personality. Neither of these can it spare and still be preaching. . . .

The truth must come truly through the person, not merely over his lips, not merely into his understanding and out through his pen or lips. It must come through his character, his affections, his whole intellectual and moral being. It must come genuinely through him. I think that, granted equal intelligence and study, here is the great difference which we find between two preachers of the Word. The Gospel has come *over* one of them and reaches us tinged and flavored with his superficial characteristics, belittled by his littleness. The Gospel has come *through* the other, and we receive it impressed and winged with all the earnestness and strength that is in him.[3]

[3] Phillips Brooks, *Lectures on Preaching* (Dutton, 1877), pp. 5, 8.

8. *Reading the Bible Aloud*

The minister has an immediate need to read the Bible well in public; he is called upon to do it at least once every Sunday. But beyond this immediate need, reading aloud offers itself as the most natural way of practicing the basic speaking skills.

Take breathing and relaxation for examples. You can practice the exercises, but how do you incorporate them into your own speaking? We suggest that you do it by way of a practice reading session of ten or fifteen minutes a day. Thus you will establish new habits in relation to continuous expression of meaningful ideas. As you read aloud, keep checking to make sure that you are inhaling properly at the pauses, and that you are not excessively tense. It will not be long before you will feel more secure about fundamental matters of relaxation and breathing. Then you can go on to another group of skills, always building upon those you have established.

GOOD READING IS LIKE TALKING

Reading out loud is an acid test of a speaker. If he can read well, he can usually speak well. But if he reads badly he still has some growing to do. The other day we heard someone remark, "It seems to me that I almost never hear the Bible read well in church. I wonder why." We began to wonder, too. We had to admit that the most interesting Bible reading we had ever heard was done by Charles Laughton one evening in a lecture series. Almost never does the reading of the Bible in church become as exciting as that. But why doesn't it?

One reason ministers read the Bible badly is that they are preoccupied with a total service of worship. They read automatically with only a fraction of their attention engaged, while the rest of their mind scouts ahead, as it were, to get ready for the next item on the order of worship. It is no great wonder, then, if the scripture is nothing but words—uninhabited by a mind or heart. Yes, quite definitely, one reason for poor scripture reading is preoccupation.

Another is familiarity. Most ministers know their Bible fairly well. They think they know the lesson for the day well enough in advance, so they do not bother to run over it. They read without rehearsing. Thus, their very familiarity with the scripture makes them read it badly.

Unconscious imitation of older ministers is another reason. All men who are now ministers once were young men sitting in the pews, listening to their elders. What is more natural than that they should read the Bible now the way they heard it then?

But even after pointing out all these reasons—preoccupation, lack of rehearsal, surface familiarity, and imitation—we have yet to state one of the most urgent difficulties. Ministers (and other speakers) do not think of public reading and public speaking in the same terms. Yet the truth is that *reading is best when it is most like talking*. The spoken word and the written word are very unlike each other, but the word that is read from a printed page—if it is read well—should sound like a spoken word. Here is the rub: On a printed page words are of equal weight and move at the same pace; spoken words are not like that at all. Some are spoken slowly and with great emphasis, others are spoken hurriedly—in fact, they are almost thrown away. Spoken words are delivered at different pitch levels and with varying volume and many pauses, long and short. None of these things can be indicated in the printing of a page, but all of them must be brought into the reading of that page through oral communication.

We repeat; good reading is like talking. It is fairly easy to write down something you have been talking about, but very hard to read something that is written so as to make it sound as if you are talking it. In fact, one of the hardest jobs in the world is to read a typed or printed page so as to make it truly come alive and sound as real as talking. Thus we come to the point: Every gain in effective public reading that we are able to consolidate will be a gain for more effective speaking. Learn the meaning of relaxation and breathing for public reading and you have learned it for speaking. Learn phrasing and emphasis, rate and range for reading and you increase your skills in these same variables for speaking.

IN THE PAUSES—BREATHE AND THINK

As you set up your working program of practice reading, you may want to browse for a while, reading here and there in the Bible and focusing mainly upon the proper use of pauses. That is, as you read, you will use each pause in two ways: (1) to inhale with the diaphragm to replenish the air supply for speech, and (2) to grasp and absorb the meaning of the next phrase before speaking it. These two simultaneous actions form the physical and mental bases of good communication. As you take in breath—at the pause —you have the air you need to produce the tone that will be used in speaking the phrase coming up. And as you grasp that next phrase (mentally)—also in the pause—you will see and feel it and you will be ready to convey it as living thought and emotion.

We falsely think of speaking and reading as an unbroken continuity, like a broad jump. It is more like leapfrog. You do not leap over the backs of ten men at once. You crouch, gathering your forces and estimating the jump; then you vault over the back of the player bending before you; again you crouch, gathering your forces and estimating the jump; then you vault. The analogy of leapfrog can be pressed too far, of course, since pauses differ from each other, some being short and others long. And in addition to the two uses we have mentioned, pauses have other uses. Nevertheless, these other uses are built upon the two primary activities—

taking in air and casting ahead to grasp the next phrase as a living unit of thought and feeling. This is where practice in reading should begin.

AIDS TO INTEGRATED READING

Next we will move on to a more integrated reading of scripture. Begin by choosing a passage which has unity within itself. This may mean ignoring verse and chapter divisions. For example, Paul's great hymn to Christian love in First Corinthians really begins with the last verse of Chapter 12. Some ministers read only the thirteenth chapter. Take another example: Jeremiah, Chapter 1, contains no less than three separate units of scripture—the data concerning the book and its author and time (1:1-3), the report of Jeremiah's first call to be a prophet (1:4-10), and the report of a second call (1:11-19). Begin by selecting a passage that is a genuine unit.

Then make sure that you have penetrated to the meaning of the passage. There may be strange words and phrases which you do not precisely understand. Look these up in a commentary. Read the passage in more than one version. Sometimes a modern speech translation is very helpful at this point.

But understanding a passage is much deeper than knowing the meaning of all its words and phrases. It involves grasping it as a unity in terms of a living historical setting. It means reliving it personally. One might even say that it means getting inside the passage so as to read it from within. Here are a few aids to that process:

1. For your own purposes boil the passage down to one sentence. What is the central truth that is being presented here?

2. Decide what type of literature this is. There are about twenty-one kinds of literature in the Bible, such as laws, poems, folk stories, history, prayers, and speeches. Certainly no minister would want to read a poem as though it were a legal statute! Nor a prayer as though it were a battle cry.

3. Learn the historical circumstances under which the passage was written—the writer, the speakers, and the purpose behind the

writing. The purpose of this study is to personalize the scripture. It is to stimulate your imagination, so that you will begin to people the scripture with live men and women and with the objects, colors, and sounds making up a real world. A man does not understand a scripture lesson as long as he is grasping it merely in intellectual terms. He has to re-create it objectively in his perceptual imagination—in other words, in a sensate manner.

4. Identify yourself with the spokesmen in the passage. To illustrate this, let us return to the first chapter of Jeremiah, mentioned a moment ago. In the first three verses, who is speaking? It seems to be the author of the book; perhaps it is the scribe, Baruch. He is writing a kind of historical preface to to the whole book of Jeremiah, telling who Jeremiah was and giving the period during which he prophesied. This was approximately the last forty or fifty years of the kingdom of Judah, before the destruction of Jerusalem and the beginning of the Babylonian Exile. To reconstruct these opening verses, therefore, we might imagine a scribe with a quill pen sitting at a table, perhaps in a room built of stone, with a small flickering oil lamp on a table. We hear his quill pen scratching on the parchment. The scribe is dressed in the costume of the sixth century before Christ. He knows that Judah is in exile, and he is writing as a fugitive who must not be discovered by the Babylonian authorities. To read that scripture appropriately, you have to imagine that you are Baruch, the scribe, in that dungeon-like room, writing under those circumstances.

Let us go on with that same first chapter of Jeremiah. The next unit is found in verses 4-10. This is a vision which took place when Jeremiah was seventeen years of age. In the vision the young Jeremiah engages in conversation with God. But look closely and you will see that Jeremiah is cast in two different roles in this scripture. On the one hand, he is a seventeen-year-old boy talking with God; on the other hand, he is a mature man telling somebody about this conversation which he held with the Almighty long years before. We may assume that Jeremiah, the old man, is dictating it to Baruch, the scribe, in the room and under the circumstances which we pictured above.

It would help us, in reading this scripture, to cast it in the form of a script for a play, something like this:

THE CALL OF JEREMIAH

[*Scene: A dungeon-like room with a bare table on which there is a single flickering oil lamp, and at which a sixth-century Palestinian scribe sits hunched over a sheet of parchment on which he is writing with a quill pen. An old, bearded man, in similar costume, paces up and down, dictating.*]

JEREMIAH (the old man): Now the word of the Lord came to me saying. . .

[*Momentarily the scene dissolves to a seventeen-year-old boy kneeling at prayer by a simple bed. An oil lamp flickers on a bedside table. It is night.*]

GOD (a strong, paternal voice; God himself invisible): Before I formed you in the womb I knew you, and before you were born I consecrated you; I appointed you to be a prophet to the nations.

JEREMIAH (the boy): Ah, Lord God! Behold, I do not know how to speak, for I am only a youth.

GOD: Do not say, "I am only a youth"; for to all to whom I send you you shall go, and whatever I command you you shall speak. Be not afraid of them for I am with you to deliver you.

[*Scene dissolves back to first, the old prophet dictating to the scribe.*]

JEREMIAH (the old man): Then the Lord put forth his hand and touched my mouth and the Lord said to me . . .

[*Scene dissolves quickly into the second, boy at bedside praying.*]

GOD: Behold, I have put my words in your mouth. See, I have set you this day over nations and over kingdoms, to pluck up and break down, to destroy and overthrow, to build and to plant.

As you read this scripture, try to create something like a play in your mind, and take the various roles, one after the other. You will identify yourself with each spokesman in turn. For instance, when you read the speeches of God, you are strong, confident, reassuring. You speak slowly with the lower tones of your pitch range. But when you are the protesting young Jeremiah, you are tense, frightened, and you speak in a higher pitch and at a rapid rate. When you are the old man Jeremiah, dictating to his scribe, you speak with a sense of awe and wonder at the glory of your calling as you look back upon it through the years. And then your quality will be somewhat breathy, your pitch low, and your rate deliberate. Of course, you do not make decisions about pitch, rate, and the like mechanically; you live your way into the role and the changes will happen.

TWO TROUBLESOME WORDS

Attention should be directed to two troublesome words in the passage just read. They are the words *saying* (1:4) and *behold* (1:6, 9). Most men emphasize these words, when they should de-emphasize them. That is, the usual way of reading these words is:

"Now the *word* of the *Lord*
came to me *saying* . . ."

Saying is emphasized. Try reading it differently. End the phrase with *me* and pause there; then couple the word *saying* with the speech of God that follows, speaking it quickly, almost as though you were not speaking it at all. The result should be something like this:

"Now the *word* of the *Lord*
came to *me*
saying *Before* I *formed* you in the womb
I *knew* you . . ."

From the above, it can be seen that the word *saying* is in a weak position; the meaning of the passage does not need the word; it could be left unsaid without altering the meaning. What havoc of meanings is wrought, then, if this very unemphatic word is emphasized.

Essentially the same thing may be said of the word *behold*. De-emphasize it. Again, let us experiment, reading a passage in two contrasting ways. First in the old way:

"*Behold*
I do not *know* how to *speak*
for I am only a *youth*."

The whole effect in such a reading is off balance. The most impressive thing in it is the sound of the word *behold*, but what are

we supposed to behold? That is lost. Now, try it another way:
"Behold *I* do not *know*
how to *speak*
for I am only a *youth*."

As we have seen, the words *saying* and *behold* are very troublesome. They have a way of throwing us off our stride and of
destroying our identification with the scriptural spokesmen. We
will learn to subordinate them, so that the personalities in and
behind the passages may speak.

PHRASING FOR READING

We have already noticed that this involves phrasing, for we
speak in phrases—in words grouped together—and not in isolated
words. It will therefore always help to divide a passage into its
constituent phrases and to decide on the important word or
words in each phrase before reading it. To do this, it will be
helpful to copy the passage.

In phrasing a selection, too, it is important to realize that phrases
differ among themselves; some are spoken quickly and with little
force, whereas others are spoken quite deliberately and with great
force. Taking all factors of phrasing into consideration, therefore,
we suggest that you make a script of the passage selected: (1) Mark
the pauses; (2) underscore the important words to be emphasized;
(3) mark the speed of each phrase, using symbols which mean *fast,
slow, normal*. (This third step will not be a continuing practice,
only in initial exercise.)

Winston Churchill, we are told, always phrased the manuscripts
of his speeches. One way of doing this is simply to put a stroke
(/) where each pause is to fall. If it is a major pause, you can use
a double stroke (//); a minor one may be indicated by a half-
stroke (').

MORE ABOUT PAUSING

Although we have already seen something of the importance of
pauses, we must realize that pauses are not just blank silences.
They are full and meaningful when properly used. A pause gives

the listener time to absorb the idea that has just been expressed in a phrase. And it gives a reader the chance to grasp a phrase as a unit in advance of delivering it, and to re-create it and individualize it as a thought. It takes time to let ideas come alive, and for both reader and speaker a pause is just that opportunity. Speakers and listeners, however, use pauses in opposite ways. For a listener a pause looks backwards; it enables him to grasp what he has just heard. For a speaker or reader a pause looks forward; it enables him to grasp what he is going to say.

But that is not all we must notice about pauses. For example, a pause may be used before an especially important word to draw attention to it—to impart an air of suspense and surprise. Suppose we take another example from Jeremiah and read the following verse to bring special emphasis to the surprising, contradictory fact that a temple has become a den of robbers:

"Has *this house*/ which is called by *my name*/ become// a *den* of *robbers* in your eyes?"// (Jeremiah 7:11.)

The pause after *become* was not necessary to the meaning, but it did help to heighten the effect of the contrast between the *house of God* and a *den of robbers*.

There are still other uses for pauses. A speaker or reader may pause for emphasis after he has said something significant which he wants us to remember. He may also pause to mark the completion of one scene or division of thought, just before he goes on to the next division of thought. For example, in reading a psalm, it is good to divide the psalm into stanzas, or strophes, and to mark the turn of thought from one strophe to the next by a major pause. A pause is a way of paragraphing or chaptering a communication. Or, to say it in dramatic language, it is the way we draw the curtain at the end of a scene.

RATING YOUR READING

From the foregoing it can be seen that the public reading of scripture can be checked against the Voice Rating Sheet. All the factors that make good speaking also make good reading. In addition, a check-up is possible—recording the scripture reading and then analyzing it by means of the rating sheet. Meanwhile, it is important to remember that a good reading of scripture, like a good speech or sermon, has to come from inside a person. He must really feel it and relive it idea by idea as he delivers it. No mechanical manipulation of voice variables will make it live. But if it is truly alive, all the voice variables will be there in strength.

It all comes down to one word: practice. If we are going to read the scripture so as to make it come alive, we must take time and thought for rehearsal. Such rehearsal could be justified on the basis of what it would do just for the public reading of the Bible. It is doubly justified when we begin to see what it can do for every kind of oral expression. To master the voice variables, practice reading the Bible aloud under criticism. Use the tape recorder, and with a companion by your side evaluate the results, going back to practice the passage again and again.

Speaking of practice, we suggest the reading of Jeremiah 26 using the script which follows.

NOTE

Remember, as you work with the script, that it is just one interpretation. You should feel free, after you get the general idea, to vary phrasing, emphasis, and rate to suit your own ideas. You might improve it considerably.

Remember, too, that the italicized words should not all be given the same value—some should have more emphasis than others, some may vary only in pitch, and others will vary in pitch plus loudness.

We have not attempted to show inflection patterns because of their highly personalized nature. As you have seen, inflections reflect feelings and attitudes no matter what the words we are speaking or reading are. Each of us has his own set of personal attitudes which will be subtly reflected as we read—no matter what patterns of phrasing and emphasis we may have followed.

If, for example, while listening to your recording of this passage, you hear to your dismay that inflections all seem to have a downward, dirge-like pattern, you will probably have to look to your feelings and attitudes for the reason—not to the script.

Feelings and attitudes are so intimately related to oral reading and speaking, as we saw in Chapter 7, they cannot be ignored in any discussion of effective public preaching or speaking.

THE TEMPLE SERMON, 608 B.C.

[*Only eleven years before the first Babylonian captivity.*
Summary: After a scathing speech against the religion of his day,
Jeremiah narrowly escapes martydom.]

[Normal]
NARRATOR: In the *beginning* of the *reign* of *Jehoiakim*/ [Fast] the son of
[Normal]
Josiah,/ *king* of Judah,/ [Slow] this *word* came from the Lord.//

[*Scene: Jeremiah's chamber, Jeremiah in prayer. The voice of God*
comes to him quietly.]

GOD (to Jeremiah alone): [S] Thus says the Lord/ [N] Stand in the *court*
of the Lord's *house*,/ [N] and *speak*/ [F] to all the *cities* of Judah which *come*
to *worship* in the house of the Lord/ [N] all the *words* that I *command*
you to speak to them;// [S] do *not hold back* a word.// [F] It *may* be/ [N] they
will *listen*,/ and everyone *turn* from his *evil* way,/ [N] that I may *repent*
of the *evil*/ [F] which I *intend* to do to *them*/ because of their *evil*
doings.// [F] You shall *say* to them . . .

[*Scene changes to the temple courts, Jeremiah addressing a throng*
or worshipers, including priests at the great altar. As Jeremiah speaks
the listeners grow increasingly angry and crowd in on the prophet
with threatening gestures.]

JEREMIAH (speaking to the unruly throng): [S] Thus *says* the Lord:/ [N] If
you will *not listen* to me,/ [F] to walk in *my law*/ [F] which I have set
before you,/ [N] and to *heed* the word of *my servants*/ [F] the *prophets*/
[N] whom I *send* to you *urgently*,/ [F] though you have *not heeded*,/ [S] then
I *will make this house* like/ [N] *Shiloh*,// [S] *and* I will make *this city*/ a
curse for *all* the *nations* of the earth.///

NARRATOR: The *priests* and the *prophets*/ and *all* the *people*/ heard Jeremiah speaking these words/ in the house of the Lord.// And when Jeremiah had *finished* speaking/ all that the Lord had commanded him to speak to all the people,/ then the *priests* and the *prophets*/ and all the *people*/laid hold of him,/

A PRIEST: saying, *You* shall *die!*// *Why* have you prophesied in the name of the Lord,/ saying, This *house* shall be like *Shiloh,*/ and this *city* shall be *desolate,*/ without *inhabitant?*//

NARRATOR: And *all* the *people*/ gathered about Jeremiah/ in the *house* of the Lord.//

[*Scene now shifts to the palace, below the temple to the south. A courier has broken from the temple throngs to run with the news to the court of the king; and court attendants soon come streaming out of the palace toward the temple.*]

NARRATOR: When the *princes* of Judah heard these things,/ they *came up* from the *king's house*/ to the *house* of the Lord/ and took their *seat* in the *entry* of the *New Gate*/ of the *house* of the Lord.// Then the *priests* and the *prophets*/ *said* to the *princes*/ and to all the *people,/*

A PRIEST: *This man*/ *deserves* the *sentence of death,*/ because he has *prophesied against this city,*/ as you have *heard* with your *own* ears.//

NARRATOR: Then *Jeremiah*/ *spoke* to all the princes and all the people,/

[*Scene: Jeremiah standing out on the temple pavement a few feet from the assembled princes, sitting in the gate, in a small semicircle.*]

JEREMIAH (making a public speech): The *Lord*/ sent me to *prophesy* against this *house* and this *city*/ *all* the words you have *heard.*// Now *therefore*/ *amend* your *ways* and your *doings*/ and *obey* the voice of the Lord *your God*,/ [S] and the Lord will *repent* of the evil/ [S] which

he has *pronounced* [F] against you.// But as for *me*,/ [F] behold, I am in

your hands./ [N] Do with me as seems *good* and *right* to you.// [N] Only/

know *for certain* that/ [F] *if* [N] you put me to *death*,/ [S] you will bring *in-*

nocent blood upon yourselves/ [N] and upon this *city* and its *inhabit-*

ants,/ [S] for in truth/ [S] the *Lord sent me to you*/ [S] to *speak all these words*

in *your ears*.// [F]

NARRATOR: Then the *princes*/ [N] and all the *people*/ [N] *said* [F] to the *priests*
and prophets,/

A PRINCE (standing up in the group): *This* [N] man/ does *not deserve* [F]

the sentence of death,/ [S] for he has *spoken* to us in the *name* of the
Lord *our God*.//

NARRATOR: And certain of the *elders* [F] of the land/ *arose* and *spoke* [F]
to all assembled people,/

AN ELDER (walking out to face the group): saying,/ [F] *Micah* [N] of More-

sheth prophesied in the days of *Hezekiah*/ [F] *king* [F] of Judah,/ and *said*
to all the people of Judah:/

[*Scene: Here imagine Micah rising specter-like out of the temple*
pavement and speaking through the elder.]

MICAH: [S] Thus says the Lord of *hosts*// [S] *Zion* shall be *plowed* as a

field;/ [S] *Jerusalem* shall become a heap of ruins,/ and the *mountain*
of the house/ a *wooded height*.//

[*Micah vanishes, and the elder continues to speak in his own right.*]

AN ELDER: Did *Hezekiah*/ [N] king of *Judah*/ [F] and all *Judah*/ [F] put *him* [N] to

death?/ [N] Did he not *fear* the *Lord*/ [N] and *entreat* the *favor* of the *Lord*,/

and did not the Lord *repent* of the evil which he had pronounced [N]

against them?// [S] But *we* are about to bring *great evil* upon ourselves.//

NARRATOR: There was *another* man/ [N] who *prophesied* [F] in the name of the Lord,/ [N] *Uriah* the son of Shemiah/ [F] from Kiriathjearim./ [N] *He* prophesied against *this city*/ [F] and against *this land*/ [N] in words *like* those of *Jeremiah*.// [F] And when *King Jehoiakim*,/ with all his warriors and all princes,/ [N] *heard* his words/ the *king* sought to put him to *death*;// [F] but when *Uriah heard* of it,/ [N] he was *afraid*/ [N] and *fled*/ [F] and escaped to *Egypt*.// [F] Then King Jehoiakim *sent* to *Egypt* certain men,/ [N] *Elnathan* the son of Achbor and *others* with him,/ [N] and they *fetched* Uriah *from* Egypt/ [F] *and* brought him *to* King Jehoiakim,/ [S] who *slew* him with the sword; and cast his *dead body* into the *burial* place of the *common* people./// [S] But the hand of *Ahikam*/ [F] the son of Shaphan/ [N] was *with Jeremiah*/ [S] so that *he* was *not given over* to the people/ [N] to be *put to death*.

If we were to cast the above scripture as a play (which is not a bad idea), we should require voices for a narrator, God, a priest, a prince, an elder, and Jeremiah—not less than six voices for one chapter. Taking each role in turn requires an alert, versatile mind—and preparation. We can begin to see what a creative job a minister could do in reading the Bible to his people, if he would only take the time to get each lesson into his system ahead of the hour of worship.

Churchgoers seldom notice the scripture reading, or listen to it. Why shouldn't we change that? Then, some Sunday morning when the sermon has missed fire, we might still have hit the target with the reading of the Bible. We have never eavesdropped on a conversation like the following, but we would like to:

"First time I ever noticed the scripture reading in a church. Usually it is just a part of the exercises and I think about something else until it's over. But not today."

"No, sir, when the preacher read the Bible today, it just seemed to come alive. It was like the TV show *You Are There.* You know,

I've never thought of this before, but if every minister could read the way ours did this morning, it would be worth while coming to church just to hear the Bible."

The quality of our sermons goes up and down, but the quality of scripture is tested by the centuries. It is never inane or trivial; it always has something to say. It is up to us to help the Bible speak— every Sunday. If we do that conscientiously for very long we will discover to our delight that the Bible is also helping us to speak.

9. The Creative Moment of Delivery

The complexity of what happens when a man stands up to preach can hardly be exaggerated. The creative moment of delivery is a time of intense integration. Think of some of the many things that have to be done, all of them at the same time: The preacher must be aware of his hearers, not in a general or confused way, but sharply enough to be able to observe and respond to their changing reactions, and to talk with them as individuals. He must know what he wants to tell these people, not for one minute but for twenty or thirty minutes, and what he has to say must be so well organized, so well thought out that it will march as a progressive development from beginning to end. The ideas must be there, vividly present in all their individuality. The structure of those ideas must be just as solidly present, so that each idea has its place in the framework of meanings. Words to clothe and convey the ideas must come out of a rich vocabulary instantly upon call. The preacher must be under an inward compulsion to share these ideas; the compulsion, in fact, must be strong enough to expel competing ideas or vagrant thoughts, producing a quality of concentration so intent upon its object that nothing will swerve it from its course until it has fulfilled its mission. The preacher's body must become a responsive instrument of his mind. His perceptual imagination must be alert. He must be in command of correct grammar and pronunciation. He must use all the voice variables. And he must communicate simultaneously on three levels —intellectual, emotional, and personal. Obviously, the creative moment of delivery is a time of intense integration.

PREPARING THE SERMON

A man will be able to bring it off consistently week after week only if he speaks out of an overflow of thought and preparation. He will constantly be trying to square his own life with his Gospel and to think his way more deeply into that Gospel for the sake of those who are in his care. He will be a conscientious student, devoting hours of every week to the next sermon.

Preparation, in general, must be of two kinds. There must be the preparation of the sermon, and there must be the preparation of the man to deliver the sermon. Or, to say it another way, the sermon must be twice born; it must be born in the study and it must be reborn in the pulpit.

The preparation of the sermon is not the province of this book, but it is fair to assume that it will require many hours of each week and that the sermon as first born in the study will be one of three things: (1) a full manuscript written verbatim as the preacher would like to deliver it, (2) a full outline which has been thought through in great detail and grasped in its entirety, or (3) a sermon fully outlined and perhaps even fully written in the mind, though none of it is committed to paper. Much is to be said for each method of preparation, but little can be said in general, for the requirements of individual speakers differ and each must find his own best way of working.

Most of us agree with Francis Bacon: "Reading maketh a full man; conference [speaking,] a ready man and writing an exact man." When a person gets his speech down on paper he can see how general it is, and he can begin to pinpoint it with specific pictures and actions; he can see how discursive it is and he can boil it down and tighten it up; he can see how confused it is and he can clarify it. Writing does something for style and for clarity of thought. Most of us find that until we have written a sermon out we have not really thought it out.

Nevertheless, a few men, strongly auditory in their thinking, do better to talk their sermons out than to write them on paper. Some men even build their sermons this way, going to a place where they talk aloud without interruption, and returning each day as the sermon grows toward its final shape. If these men want the sermon in manuscript, they simply make a tape recording or dictate it and have it transcribed. Once they have the manuscript in hand, they can criticize or rewrite just as anyone else would do.

Probably all speakers need the discipline of writing and rewriting; but each man must work at it in his own way. Some will do better to write before preaching. Others will get more from writing afterwards.

PREPARING THE MAN

So much for the first step, preparing the sermon. Now we have to prepare the man to deliver that sermon. The preparation of the sermon—especially if it has been thorough—may work subtly against the preparation of the man. This is where he has to be on guard. Having "finished" his sermon, he relaxes and sits back, feeling that he is "all ready for Sunday." But there is still some time until Sunday, and the sermon which is so vivid and exciting to him now, so much a part of him and so internal to his thought and feeling, may become external by Sunday morning.

Or another subtle danger may interpose itself: The well-prepared sermon may become an object of art in the preacher's eyes and he may succumb to the temptation of delivering it for its own sake. The better the sermon the greater is this temptation. We cannot tell ourselves too often that the sermon is not the words written on paper. Nor is it the words spoken in the sanctuary. It is the message that gets through to the hearers. Or, to put it in a figure, it is the electric spark that leaps from the pulpit to the pew; it is neither in the pulpit nor in the pew, but between them.

Seen in this light, no "sermon" is fully prepared in the study.

Everything that goes before the creative moment of delivery itself is preliminary and instrumental to the real sermon, the communicated word spoken in the midst of the people. Even the full manuscript is preliminary and instrumental. The most polished sermon is unfinished until it has been delivered.

The sermon itself is a fleeting and evanescent thing, depending upon the instant in which each word is spoken to come alive and quicken life. In this respect it is perhaps like the electric spark that ignites the vaporized gasoline in the cylinder of an automobile. The progress of the car is caused by nothing but a series of such sparks igniting gasoline, and the whole object of the expendable gasoline and the fleeting spark is to propel the car down the highway. All a minister's preparation in the study is nothing better than a supply of expendable gasoline to be used up by the igniting spark of creative delivery; and its object is not to preserve itself but to deliver the power needed to move the people toward God.

The practical upshot of what we have been saying is that a minister must devote an hour or two on Saturday evening or on Sunday morning to his preparation for delivery. Let him make sure that he gets a full night's sleep, that he comes to the pulpit in good health and in full vigor. We have seen that a man delivers his sermon with his whole body; it is important that he be physically keen. Let him also exclude unnecessary distractions, competing thoughts, or interests that may veto the concern of the sermon. Let him concentrate upon this one thing, bring all his powers to bear at this one point. Only so can there be the genuine integration upon which creative delivery depends.

In the time which he has at his disposal for his preparation to deliver, a minister has the following things to accomplish: He must grasp the organization of his sermon as a living whole, moving to climax. He must become keenly sensitive to the thesis or proposition which he hopes to establish, and no less keenly aware of the object of his sermon, the target he wants to hit. And he must master the content, the specific material of the sermon, or devise an adequate system of notes by which he can carry it with him and have it readily available in the instant of his need.

To accomplish these ends, there are many different ways of working. A man may speak from a skeleton of key words and phrases (little resembling a formal outline); he may speak from a full outline; or he may speak without notes of any kind. Every man should find his own best method by trial and error over a considerable period of time, always checking his own judgment by that of one or more friends. Any man will do well to vary his method from time to time so as to develop a feeling of freedom and mastery in any and all situations. A man will do better with any method when he knows that it is not his only method.

Now, let us look at a few alternatives.

FROM MANUSCRIPT TO NOTES

The great Frederick W. Robertson of Brighton used this method. He himself said of it:

The word *extempore* does not exactly describe the way I preach. I first make copious notes; then draw out a form (rough plan); afterwards write copiously, sometimes, twice or thrice, the thoughts, to disentangle them and arrange them in a connected whole; then make a syllabus, and, lastly a skeleton which I take into the pulpit.[1]

S. Parkes Cadman of Brooklyn wrote his sermons in longhand and made an abstract of notes for the pulpit.[2] Harry Emerson Fosdick before his retirement reported rather cryptically that he wrote a full manuscript, drew off an outline, and spoke from it as he was able.[3] Eugene Carson Blake reports more fully that he writes on Friday and reads the entire manuscript to his wife that evening. On Saturday he consumes three or four hours typing full notes which amount to a rewriting of the sermon. He then reads it late Saturday evening, and again (aloud) early Sunday, and preaches from rather full notes.[4] Harold Chandler Robbins reported that he

[1] Albert H. Currier, *Nine Great Preachers* (Pilgrim Press, 1912), p. 264.
[2] Harold A. Prichard, *The Minister, the Method, the Message* (Scribner's, 1932), pp. 157-158.
[3] *Ibid.*, pp. 169-170.
[4] Donald MacLeod (ed.), *Here Is My Method* (Revell, 1952), pp. 26-27.

wrote in full, revised, and then abstracted a few key words that would fit into the palm of his hand.[5]

For those who may care to use this method the following steps are suggested:

Step 1. Make a skeleton of key words and phrases. Even manuscript preachers seldom read their compositions word for word. Instead, their eyes dart down to pick up certain key words and phrases—perhaps underscored—a few to a paragraph. All we have to do to get away from manuscript, then, is to lift these key words and phrases out and set them upon a separate piece of paper. Quotations which need to be delivered verbatim may be copied in full, but for most ideas sentences are unnecessary. A word will often summon a whole paragraph. (See p. 111 for an example of this kind of speaking notes.)

Step 2. Read the manuscript aloud. Do this, when possible, on the day of delivery three or four hours before time. Do not read it hypnotically or by rote, but read to think it through no less than three times. (See pp. 148-151). Read it a second time, paying close attention to the wholeness of the message, the major divisions of thought, and the main emphasis. And read it yet a third time, with a view to communicating it to those who will shortly hear it. Some men do this third reading in the pulpit from which they expect to deliver it, arriving at the church early enough to do so without auditors.

Step 3. Lay the manuscript aside and re-create the sermon, using the skeleton of key words and phrases which you made in step 1. If the skeleton fails you at any point, add the necessary words to fill the gaps. Go through the entire sermon in this way, silently or aloud.

Step 4. Put aside both manuscript and skeleton notes; outline the sermon from memory with emphasis upon the main divisions. This will show you that you grasp your message as a whole and are ready to share it.

Step 5. Forget it. Put a cushion of time between your practice

[5] Prichard, *op. cit.*, p. 155.

and your delivery, at least two hours if possible. Otherwise you may over-prepare and "go stale."

FROM MANUSCRIPT TO NO NOTES

Many celebrated ministers have gone to the pulpit without notes of any kind even though they took pains to write the sermon in full manuscript. Among these are Walter Russell Bowie, James Gordon Gilkey, Clarence E. Macartney, John A. Redhead, Jr., and Ralph W. Sockman. Dr. Bowie dictates in full on Wednesday or Thursday of each week; he prefers this method of composition because the rhythm of the spoken voice stimulates his thoughts. When the manuscript comes from the typist he then reads it several times with great care and concentration. When he preaches, it is without manuscript or notes of any kind.[6] Dr. Gilkey confesses that his rehearsal includes preaching the sermon several times to the furniture of his study.[7] Dr. Macartney, who has written a book in support of preaching without notes (see Bibliography), writes no less than four drafts of his sermon; he keeps simplifying it until he has reduced it to a few heads. He dictates the sermon in full to a typist; then he reads the manuscript several times. Finally he makes a brief outline which he commits to memory. Quotations are memorized verbatim.[8] Dr. Redhead types his own manuscript, completing it by Friday noon. To absorb the sermon for delivery, he reads it twice Saturday morning, then goes over it in his mind. He reads it again before breakfast Sunday, and preaches without notes.[9] Dr. Sockman writes a manuscript, which he reads Saturday night before retiring. Then on Sunday at seven o'clock in the morning he "thinks it through for about an hour and a half before breakfast." He takes no manuscript into the pulpit, but he does take the quotations.[10]

The following steps are suggested as a way of working from full manuscript to a delivery which is completely free of notes:

[6] *Ibid.*, pp. 167-168.
[7] MacLeod, *op. cit.*, pp. 71-72.
[8] *Ibid.*, pp. 111-112.
[9] *Ibid.*, pp. 154-155.
[10] *Ibid.*, pp. 182-183.

Step 1. Make your skeleton of notes as simple as possible, using an absolute minimum of key words set in a bold outline. The sharper the outline the more memorable it will be. Keep paring your notes to the bone.

Steps 2 and 3 are identical with those in the preceding section.

Step 4. Commit the skeleton to memory and, placing it in a pocket from which you may quickly retrieve it in case of emergency, rehearse the sermon from beginning to end. Then forget it until the time of delivery.

Those desiring other procedures can work out their own methods on the basis of the ways of working seen in the five ministers whom we have presented in the paragraphs above. Many ministers do write in full and then preach without notes.

FROM A WRITTEN OUTLINE

Extemporaneous speaking—always to be distinguished from impromptu speaking—usually begins with a written outline prepared rather fully. But even here it is a mistake to suppose that the sermon is ready for delivery when the outline is written.

Making no notes all through the week, Henry Ward Beecher entertained several sermons which were growing in various stages of development until Sunday morning, when he chose the one that was ripest; he then prepared a full outline, sketching it rapidly.[11] John Short of Toronto, Canada, works from a summary of notes prepared on Thursday or Friday; he progressively reduced this summary to a very few notes, making the last summary on Saturday evening, or even as late as nine o'clock Sunday morning.[12] The late Charles Reynolds Brown, having begun his career as a court reporter, followed the habit of writing and making his notes in shorthand. As described to his students at Yale, his method went something like this: The notes on which he depended for delivery were composed on three of the twice-folded sections of a regular sheet of typing paper; these he placed in the pocket of his suit as he spoke from memory. Somewhat similarly, Robert Norwood of

11 Currier, op. cit., p. 344.
12 MacLeod, op. cit., p. 170.

St. Bartholomew's in New York used to prepare by thinking all week about his sermon, much as Beecher did; then toward the end of the week he prepared two sheets of yellow paper, talking to himself all the while.[13]

Here is a suggested method of speaking extemporaneously, from notes:

Step 1. Using the outline which you have prepared, silently think your speech or sermon through from beginning to end, making sure that your ideas are concrete and vivid to you. If you come upon sections that are abstract or general, stop to work with them until you can perceptualize them or illustrate them.

Step 2. Lay the outline aside and reproduce its main divisions from memory. Also indicate your major illustrations of each main point.

Step 3. Rehearse the whole sermon aloud, using your written outline as a guide.

Step 4. Put a cushion of one or two hours between step 3 and delivery.

FROM MEMORIZED OUTLINE, WITHOUT NOTES

An extemporaneous speech without notes may be put together by gradually talking it out over a period of days until it emerges as a whole—depending on notes at no point in the development. It is all "done in the head." Apparently this is the way John Calvin worked, for it is reported of him: "He made no notes of his preparation, but stored his thoughts in his admirable memory until he needed them in the pulpit."[14] Alexander MacLaren worked in much the same way, for he said of his own method:

I began my ministry with the resolution that I would not write my sermons, *but would think and feel them,* and I have stuck to it ever since. It costs quite as much time in preparation as writing, and a far greater expenditure of nervous energy in delivery, but I am sure that it is best for me, and equally sure that everybody has to find out his own way.[15]

[13] Prichard, *op. cit.,* pp. 174-176.
[14] T. H. L. Parker, *Oracles of God* (London: Lutterworth, 1947), p. 69.
[15] Currier, *op. cit.,* p. 289.

MacLaren modified the method only at one point; he did make some jottings and even wrote out some sentences. The late Joseph Fort Newton, however, followed the no-writing program all the way. His preparation was done wholly by process of mental composition—in great detail, nonetheless. He then wrote a manuscript of his sermon after he had delivered it.[16] Bishop Gerald Kennedy closely approximates Newton's method. Beginning with a few notes on Wednesday morning, he goes to a room where he can talk the sermon out, returning to amplify and complete it by speaking it on Thursday, Friday, Saturday, and Sunday mornings. The Sunday morning out-loud rehearsal may include only parts of the sermon.[17]

FROM MANUSCRIPT

Many men prefer to take the full manuscript into the pulpit. Even then, preparation for delivery is necessary. In most cases this will take the form of reading the manuscript aloud several times. (This reading will follow essentially the same lines as suggested in Step 2 of "From Manuscript to Notes" on p. 102 above.) Mere familiarity with the words of the manuscript is not enough. There must be a grasp of the whole movement of the sermon's organized thought; its object and aim must be there to center the sermon on its target. At the same time, the details of the sermon must be vivid—living in perceptual imagination and experienced as a moving procession of colorful images. Yet again, the manuscript must be read as communication to persons. In general, it seems wisest to rehearse the manuscript aloud with a different one of these purposes in mind for each reading: once for perceptual creativity; once for organization, unity, aim; once for communication to persons.

In the pulpit a given minister will handle the manuscript in one of two ways. He will either read it verbatim or merely refer to it, relying upon it no more than upon a rather full set of notes. In other words, he will read it or he will preach from it. Thomas Chalmers is an example of the first practice. Not only did he read

<hr>

[16] Prichard, *op. cit.*, p. 179.
[17] MacLeod, *op. cit.*, pp. 94-95.

his sermon word for word, but he held the manuscript in his left hand and slavishly followed each word with the index finger of his right hand! Nevertheless, as he got into the sermon, one hearer reported, "His whole being seemed to rush into his preaching." Another said, "His eyes were afire with intelligence and rapture and zeal."[18] Charles Clayton Morrison, former editor of the *Christian Century* and Yale lecturer (*What Is Christianity?*), has moved thousands with his impassioned reading of a manuscript from which he scarcely lifted his eyes.

One can think of numerous preachers who make the second use of a manuscript; for them it becomes a kind of road map, to be consulted as needed but not to be followed slavishly. George A. Buttrick influenced a whole generation of seminary students toward this method by the spell which he wove over those who heard his Yale lectures, *Jesus Came Preaching*. His masterful handling of his manuscripts was a work of art.

Nevertheless, the use of full manuscript is only for a gifted and exceptional few. Any man who is drawn to this method should check and double check with trusted hearers and through tape recording to discover how well he is doing it, and to make sure that directness of communication is not suffering.

We have been interested recently in reading several ministers' reasons for preaching from full manuscript. One of them says, ". . . If one has written a sermon in full and taken time and trouble to get it right inside it, he is far from being tied to his manuscript; and it is a great comfort to the preacher, and to the more thoughtful type of congregation, that he has his manuscript in front of him."[19]

Another minister justifies his use of full manuscript upon other grounds: "I know that many prefer me to preach without manuscript," he writes, "but I always know that I say more in a given number of minutes, say it with greater precision and in defter sentences, than when I let myself go without it. No doubt there is

---

[18] Ilion T. Jones, *Principles and Practice of Preaching* (Abingdon, 1956), p. 194.

[19] Roderick Bethune in MacLeod, *op. cit.*, p. 15.

a liberty, a face-to-face address, a directness that folks feel is impeded when a preacher has his manuscript."[20]

These two quotations are fairly representative of ministers who use manuscripts in the pulpit; they suggest two main arguments for this practice: One, it gives the minister himself greater security. Two, it enables him to be more precise in his language. A little reflection suggests that these arguments are probably more impressive to ministers than they are to the people in the congregation. Most people do not seem to care whether a minister feels secure and comfortable about his sermon. They are more interested in his feeling excited about it; they want him to tell them about it face to face. Neither do they seem to care for his language to be polished like a gem if he has achieved the polish at the expense of freshness and vitality.

Because of the mixed emotions involved, no man is his own best judge of the effectiveness of his own manuscript preaching. He may feel that he is more communicative, when he is only more grammatical. Meantime, freshness, directness, vitality languish and the people fail to listen. Other things being equal, a manuscript in the pulpit is justified only if we have proved by trial and error that it is our most effective method of delivery. We should do it only after repeated experiments in a more direct method. Even then, we should do it only with the advice of discriminating friends who will help us judge our comparative effectiveness.

EYE CONTACT

To speak effectively to people we must "look them in the eye." This means not simply staring at them, but *seeing* them so as to receive the visual messages which they send us. Except for the gifted few who have mastered the art of reading their manuscripts, the minister who speaks without some eye contact is speaking with only a fraction of his power. This is one reason why people always appreciate a speaker who uses no notes.

Nevertheless, there are ways of using notes which minimize the breaking of eye contact. It goes without saying that notes should

[20] Henry Sloan Coffin in MacLeod, *op. cit.*, p. 58.

be simple, legible, and readable at a glance. Thoroughly familiar with them, a speaker can consult them without breaking communication. This means that he will glance at his notes, not in the pauses and transitions when he has stopped speaking momentarily, but when looking just a step ahead while he is talking. Thus he will have continuous communication with the congregation—communication by eye while pausing and most of the time while speaking, communication by ear during the brief times when eye contact is interrupted. If a speaker stops speaking to look down at his notes, he will spasmodically break all contact with his hearers, and his speech will lurch along by fits and jerks.

Consulting notes is less distracting if the speaker does not stand directly over them so that he has to bob his head up and down like a drinking hen. By standing back a step or two from the pulpit desk he will eliminate most of this. The notes will then be more nearly in the line of vision with the people. The speaker simply casts his eye down to the paper, meantime keeping his head up and facing his hearers.

As for the breaking of eye contact to stare at the ceiling or the floor or the wall, there is no excuse except habit—a bad habit. To speak with people effectively we must "look them in the eye."

LEARNING FROM INFORMAL TALKS

A pet complaint of ministers is that people often seem to like their informal talks better than their Sunday morning sermons. This does not mean that the informal talks are better in themselves but it suggests that they are probably more direct, more spontaneous and alive. Ministers tend to minimize their informal talks and to regard them as less effective than their highly polished sermons.

Perhaps a reversal is in order. Let the manner, the ease and freedom of the informal talks become the norm for the delivery of the sermon—not for its matter but for its manner. The real norm of good pulpit communication is not in the stiff formality so widely in evidence at eleven o'clock on Sunday morning, but in lively give-and-take. And when this begins to happen we will be less concerned with paper and more concerned with men's hearts.

The following examples are given to illustrate the types of outlines we have been discussing.

From Manuscript to Delivery

A *Skeleton of Key Words for Use in the Pulpit*

Introduction

    A. Irony . . . Moses never set foot . . . original vision . . . aroused . . . unified . . . Sinai, 40 yrs. . . . desert sands—fertile hills. Deut. 34:1-5. ʻ

    B. Unjust? Every man is Moses. Ministers.

Body

  I. True in counseling. Jordan of decision . . . rapids . . . Jericho . . . Joshua of self-determination. Seem cruel . . . you roused him. Nevertheless . . . "Thou shalt not pass over . . ."

  II. Pulpit . . . Mt. Nebo. Spy out . . . valleys, peaks (etc.).

A *Written Outline—For Extemporaneous Speaking*

Introduction

    A. The irony: Moses who freed Israel could not accompany his people into Canaan.

      1. His act of emancipation.

      2. His leadership for forty years.

      3. His death on Nebo. Deut. 34:1-5.

    B. The seeming injustices: Every man repeats Moses' story, including ministers.

Body

  I. The truth as seen in personal counseling.

    A. Can accompany friend only so far. Ill. To Jordan.

    B. His insight and freedom must be his own. Ill. The analogies to entering Canaan.

  II. The truth as seen in preaching (etc.).

Minimum Outline to Be Memorized—For Speaking Without Notes

Introduction

    A. Moses: leaving Egypt . . . denied Canaan. Deut. 34:1-5. (Read from Bible.)

    B. We: like Moses.

Body

  I. Counseling.

  II. Preaching (etc.).

The opening paragraphs of the speech which is the basis of the three treatments presented follows. The incomplete outline samples represent only the content of these paragraphs.

The View from Mount Nebo

It seems a cruel irony of biblical history that Moses never set foot in the Promised Land. It was Moses who saw the original vision of national freedom, who aroused the Israelites out of the torpor of slavery, unified them into a nation, gave them their laws at Sinai. Through all forty years of the wilderness wandering, it was Moses who kept pointing beyond the desert sands to the fertile hills of Canaan. But he never climbed those hills. Instead . . . "Moses went up from the plains of Moab unto Mount Nebo, to the top of Pisgah, which faces Jericho. And the Lord showed him all the land . . . and the Lord said to him, This is the land, which I have sworn to Abraham, Isaac, and Jacob, saying, To thy seed will I give it. Now I have caused thee to see it with thine eyes, but thou shalt not pass over into it. So Moses, the servant of God, died there in the land of Moab . . ." (Deut. 34:1-5).

It seems unjust, but such is life. Someone has said that every man is a Moses who dies outside his Promised Land. This includes ministers. The best we can achieve in the leadership of our people is a view from Mount Nebo. We cannot cross the Jordan with them or go with them into their Canaan.

This is true in personal counseling. You can walk with your friend to the Jordan of his own personal decision, but you may go no further. He must wade the rapids of this river alone, and go on to storm his own Jericho without you. And if you have done your work well, he will not look back; for he will not need you any more. This may seem cruel and hard, for you may have been the one who roused your friend out of the torpor of slavery and set his feet in the way of Canaan. Nevertheless, the Lord says to you as he did to Moses, "Thou shalt not go over this Jordan."

The pulpit, too, is a kind of Mount Nebo. You stand there on that eminence and spy out the land for all your people, and you send them out to march down its valleys and scale its peaks, but the choice of the valleys and the peaks is theirs, not yours . . . (And so forth.)

10.   A Suggested Guide for
Classes and Workshops

Teachers of seminary classes will want to work out their own methods of instructing students in the elements of creative sermon delivery discussed in the nine previous chapters of this book. But for those informal classes and workshops which may be set up by ministers themselves and conducted with little or no professional guidance, a few rather specific suggestions seem to be in order. If seminary teachers also find the suggestions useful, the helps will be doubly justified.

WHY WORK WITH A GROUP?

Early in this book a base line was laid down: If you want to improve your sermon delivery, learn how to listen analytically, both to others and to yourself. Undeniably, the best conditions for doing both kinds of listening are those provided by a good class or workshop. A man can work alone—as can be seen from the detailed steps of Chapter 11—but he will work better and faster as a member of a harmonious group.

The reasons are quickly apparent. To begin with, a speaker will be helped by his fellows to objectify his listening. While he is alone he can excuse and rationalize his faults, or miss them altogether; but he cannot long dismiss them in the face of the united testimony of ten or twelve fellow preachers. He will be brought to face them squarely. Moreover, his work-mates will see possibilities and make suggestions for improvement which may never have occurred to him alone. In other words, he will have a whole group teaching him, not merely one man; and he will learn more because he has more teachers.

But this is not all. He will also learn by listening to and criticizing the preaching of the other members of the group. He will learn by being forced to analyze their faults and their virtues and by having to report his findings and check them against the judgments of his classmates. He will learn as he strives constructively to help each of the other members of his group to find his own key to better preaching. In short, he will learn from what he seeks to impart.

Still further, as the class achieves group solidarity, that mysterious activity which the psychologists call *transference* will begin to take place. Each member of the class will begin to identify with the others and to learn from their positive and negative examples. Thus when one man preaches the others are not simply audience but actively participating speakers. In a word, they are speaking and learning vicariously. The group itself teaches its own members.

WORKING TOGETHER

1. Begin by forming a class or workshop. It should be large enough to provide variety and spark enthusiasm; it should be small enough to promote group feeling and give opportunities for frequent speaking. These conditions are usually fulfilled by a class of ten or twelve members. If no instructor is available, someone will have to serve as chairman; this can be a rotating responsibility.

2. Find a meeting place. Since this is to be a class in preaching, the ideal setting would be the sanctuary of a church or chapel. In any case, it should be a hall large enough to require the volume to which a preacher must become accustomed in speaking to his morning congregation. A small classroom will not do nearly so well.

3. Promote group solidarity. Members of the class must come to know each other well; but, more important, they must come to like and trust one another. It is not enough that they should be polite and outwardly friendly. Politeness can be the armor of subtle hostility and defensiveness. The class is not a group until it can achieve some of the freedom and candor that characterize a good family. This will not happen right at the beginning; group relationships grow. But there are ways of nourishing these relationships so that they grow more easily.

One good way to begin is to assign short impromptu speeches all around. Let each man talk not more than four minutes, preferably about himself. This will lessen the anxiety of each toward the first sermon he is to deliver to the group; it will provide a short road to mutual acquaintance; and, if the Voice Rating Sheet (Appendix A) is used, it will serve as a preliminary exercise in ear training.

It is also wise to spend a little time in direct discussion of what it means to work together, to achieve group solidarity. The first hurdle will be to banish competitiveness. It will be hard, especially at first, to keep members from comparing themselves with each other and from entering the class as contestants vying for top honors. The habits of our competitive society, though foreign to the Christian faith, are hard even for ministers to shed. But every effort must be made to shed them. Let it be made clear at the very beginning that each must find the way of preaching that is uniquely suited to him. No preacher is meant to be a carbon copy of another. He should measure himself, not against his fellows, but against his own inherent best; and he must find his own style within his own experience. In other words, let each member of the class be encouraged to be a genuine individual.

It should also be clear that each member of the class has a responsibility in every session, not only on those days when he himself is preaching. He is there to help the others to find their own particular style. This means candid criticism from a constructive purpose. When is it dangerous to criticize negatively? When it affords the critic pleasure! When is it safe? When, even though it is painful to the critic, it devolves upon him as his personal responsibility to his friend.

When a class or workshop achieves a genuine solidarity, the members will all pull for each other. Normally, this may not appear until the beginning of the second round of sermons. By that time competitive and defensive states of mind should be giving way to genuine mutuality. No one should try to be the star. None should gloat over the failure or confusion of another. Any man's failures will be in some measure the failures of the whole group, and any man's successes will be the success of all. There should be criticism, always candid, sometimes sharp, but it should be given always to help, never to destroy. Such a group working together over a period of several days or weeks can prove itself to be a dynamic teaching instrument.

4. Establish a speaking order and set up a preaching schedule. Each man should be given a number of preaching opportunities. Experience in one seminary over a number of years has tended to show that the ideal number is five sermons by each class member, taken in turn. Four fall just a bit short of enabling a man to get into his stride and find his way to a measure of mastery. The sixth seems to add nothing that was not achieved by the fifth.

5. Provide each member with a specific listening assignment. The assignments may be taken from the three rating sheets in Appendix A and may follow a pattern something like this:

    a. Pitch, with its four constituent elements.

    b. Quality.

    c. Articulation.

    d. Pronunciation.

    e. Rate, with special attention to flexibility or change of pace.

    f. Volume and emphasis.

    g. Phrasing and use of pauses.

    h. Mastery of notes.

    i. Physical action, including gesture and mannerisms.

    j. Immediate feelings: audience rapport, creativity, preparedness, self-confidence, will to communicate.

    k. Deep, persistent feelings.

Each of these eleven topics, with subtopics, can be placed on a card, and the cards will be distributed at the beginning of each session, rotating assignments from session to session.

An alternative procedure would be to mimeograph copies of the three rating sheets in Appendix A and supply every member with one of each, to be filled out at the conclusion of the sermon.

Under either alternative, every member of the class should be listening with a kind of binaural attention. He will be hearing the sermon as a whole at the same time that he is listening for his particular assignment. This sounds more complicated than it is. But, to make it sound just a bit more complicated, this word should be added: Let each listener give his attention to the preacher; as much as possible, let him avoid obvious note-taking while the delivery is in progress. Such notes as are necessary can be exceedingly brief; most things can be remembered and entered on paper at the close of the sermon. The speaker needs the help of your attentive response.

6. Let each speaker preach a complete sermon for each appearance, a sermon such as he would offer to his Sunday morning congregation. There is something crucial about such a communication; a man puts more into it, counts upon it more than upon his casual speeches. Short talks and incidental speeches will almost certainly fail to expose a speaker's real problems, whereas a full-scale sermon has a way of bringing nearly all of them into the open. Many speakers do not swing into their typical delivery until they are "fairly under way" and talking "in deadly earnest."

7. Make a tape recording of each sermon as it is being delivered. The machine should be as inconspicuous as possible. If only the microphone can be in evidence, so much the better.

8. Following the sermon, gather the class at the front of the hall and discuss the sermon as a group for at least half an hour. Each person will report on his assignment, the class reacting freely. At the end of the discussion the chairman or instructor should summarize the speaker's points of strength and weakness. The preacher should emerge from such a session knowing what his chief problems are and with some decisions about those that are

uppermost. These are his possible growing edges, his personal frontiers.

LISTENING TO THE TAPE RECORDING

The procedure which we have just outlined will be highly beneficial to any preacher without the seventh step, but with it much more becomes possible. We shall assume that the whole class will not listen as a group to any recording. The purpose behind making it is to enable a man to hear himself. Thus we come to our next step:

9. At a later hour in the day, the preacher will sit down and listen to his tape-recorded sermon in the light of the class discussion. He can do this alone, but he will get more from his listening if he has someone by his side, the instructor or another member of the class who heard the sermon in "live" delivery. If questions of rate or pitch are involved, it will be helpful to stop the tape at the pauses for a number of phrases to study time patterns or pitch patterns. If problems of articulation are at issue, all offending words and phrases should be listed as they appear. One of the values of working with a recorded speech is that the tape can be played again and again or parts of it repeated as various elements are studied and analyzed in turn.

The session at the recording machine may be extended, especially if preacher and companion fall into a discussion of deep and persistent feelings disclosed by the class's rating of emotions. This should be regarded as a counseling opportunity; it can be an hour of revelation and a point of new beginnings. It can lead to other sessions in which self-understanding and self-acceptance are sought at deeper levels. Often such a session at the recorder leads to interviews with a personal counselor. Such a follow-up should be expected and encouraged.

INDIVIDUAL DRILL AND PRACTICE

Now you have been pushed out upon your own personal frontier. Whether you make anything of it depends upon the regularity and persistence of your practice. We assume that you will emerge from the class sessions and from listening to your tape-recorded sermon with an agenda of your own speech difficulties, grouped by their natural clusterings. (See p. 39.)

10. Using the exercises in Appendix C and the directions of the text, work to master each problem. Repeat the exercises daily throughout the duration of the class or workshop; determine to continue them for at least several months into the future. Old habits have to be broken; new habits have to be formed. This means repetition, frequent and persistent repetition, until gains have been incorporated into the automatic nervous system.

11. Incorporate your improvements into daily conversational talk. The reasons are simple: (a) Here you may correct yourself without embarrassment. (b) Conversation makes up the bulk of our weekly talking; the habits of conversation can be made to support our public speaking. If we are talking well day by day there is a good chance that we will talk well on Sunday. This applies especially to pronunciation and articulation, but it applies effectively at most other points as well. (See point 9 in the next chapter for a fuller discussion of this step.)

12. Test and consolidate the integration of your speaking skills by reading the Bible aloud every day. Since reading aloud is best when it is most like talking, the skills of good reading contribute to good speaking. Therefore, practice reading aloud with a view to using all the voice variables and all the factors of creative thought and feeling which this book has presented.

The rest will be a by-product. Given time and patience your drill and practice will carry over into increased pulpit effectiveness.

ADDENDUM

Although we have excluded from this book all consideration of sermon content and organization, there is no reason why a class or workshop in preaching should limit itself so narrowly. We have refrained from discussing other topics in the present volume because we wanted to devote our space to the more neglected subjects we have presented, and also because questions of content and organization are adequately covered in a number of books on sermon preparation. In cases where it is desirable to work at all elements in the spoken sermon, including content and organization, it will be simple to assign the topics of oral delivery to three or four people rather than to the whole class, thus leaving the other members free to discuss such topics as illustrations, organization, diction, grammar, relevance to human need, theological insight, etc. It is obvious, too, that various clusterings of topics can be taken up in series and that it is not necessary to consider them all simultaneously. Thus, for example, the first few sessions of a course may be devoted to sermon organization, the next few to content, and the final sessions to oral delivery. Widening the purpose of the class or workshop in this manner will not change the fundamental method outlined above.

11. *A Self-Help Program for Individuals*

This chapter is addressed to the reader who is out of seminary, sufficiently far from preaching clinics and workshops to need an individual way of working. Of course, it is often possible for ministers to form their own workshops through the auspices of ministerial retreats, adult conferences, or ministerial associations. So the fact that there is no seminary near at hand and that no class opportunities are provided does not prevent a group of ministers from doing something for themselves in their own vicinity. If all these resources fail, however, an individual minister can still map out a program for his own growing effectiveness in the delivery of sermons. We offer here such a program; it unfolds in twelve steps:

1. Acquaint yourself with the fundamental factors in effective speech. This means simply to read and digest the first nine chapters of this book.

2. Sharpen your ear by listening to and rating other speakers.

a. Use the rating sheets to score other speakers. The simplest thing to do is to mimeograph the rating sheets in Appendix A so that you will have one of each for each speech you hear. We know, of course, that you will not be free to give this treatment to every speech made in your presence; nevertheless there will be many opportunities. Do not overlook radio and television speakers.

b. Listen to voice, not to content. To rate a speech on the voice variables it will be necessary to alter your listening habits. Ordinarily you probably listen to what a speaker is saying. If you notice how he is speaking you do so only with marginal attention, unless, of course, his method is so obstructive that it draws attention to itself. You will have to change all that for the time being. Stop listening to the content of the speech and start listening to the voice variables and other factors of speaking manner.

c. Listen selectively to a few factors at a time. Listen selectively, taking from one to three factors at a time and then passing on to another group. Before long you will be able to increase your span of attention and hear several more factors at a given time, but it is well to begin simply.

d. When possible, record the speech. One good way of solving the problem of separating content from method in listening to a speech, where it is feasible, is to record the speech. Listen to it for content when you hear it the first time. Then go back and listen to the voice factors indicated. It will be simple, for example, to have a radio repairman fit your radio with a phono output jack which can be plugged directly into the radio input of your tape recorder. We are assuming that you will get a tape recorder with good fidelity and use it faithfully. It is indispensable to the program upon which you are embarking.

e. First comes a good ear, then a good voice. We would suggest that you score no less than ten speeches by as many different speakers as possible before you turn to an analysis of your own. A cultivation of a good speaking voice depends upon the acquiring of a good ear. And ears have to be trained.

3. Begin recording your own speeches. It is, of course, impossible for anyone to hear himself as others hear him; but the invention of tape recording has now made it possible for a person to come remarkably close to doing so, if certain precautions are taken. In these days it should be unthinkable that anyone who speaks pro-

fessionally should not take advantage of this opportunity to hear himself and improve himself.

Record all kinds of speeches under a variety of circumstances. Get as faithful a record as you can of your speaking voice in all kinds of situations—the Sunday sermon, by all means; but also the informal talk, the round-table discussion, personal conversations, and even the church announcements. Sometimes a man's trouble centers in the fact that he has two kinds of speech, one public, the other private. When this happens, it is usually his private voice that should set the norm for the public one. No man will believe this of himself until he actually hears that his private speaking is more alive and more interesting.

4. Enlist the help of a trusted friend. For reasons already set forth, subjective elements make it difficult for a man to hear himself accurately if he listens alone. He needs someone with whom to check his judgments. If he can check with several people, that is even better.

a. Your helper should be a true friend. The only helpful relationship in such an enterprise is a permissive one, so there can be complete candor and unself-conscious give-and-take.

b. Your wife may also help, but in a limited way. She will help you all she can, of course, but she is emotionally identified with you to such an extent that her listening may be only a little more helpful than your own. You need your wife's help; but you probably also need another listener as well.

c. Get a friend who can stay with you over a period of several weeks or months. Many men in your community could fill the role. The one you choose may be a fellow minister, or a lawyer, or a schoolteacher. Look over your community and you will find him, for he is almost certainly there. Much can be done in two or three months; more will be done in about a year. Your voice problems were slow in accumulating. Do not be discouraged if they resist attack for a while.

5. Make a complete analysis of your speaking voice. Using the Voice Rating Sheet, you and your friend should listen to and rate

your speech independently, then compare notes. Include the emotional factors and do not pull back from questions about personality.

After the initial analysis, continue to make checkups every few months during the period of practice.

Great care should be exercised in making this analysis. The diagnosis will determine the cure, and if the diagnosis is incorrect the cure will be ineffectual. In one instance it may even be harmful; we refer to incorrect judgment about pitch level. Suppose you decide—erroneously—that your pitch level is too high. Thereupon you set to work to lower it, thus straining your vocal cords and producing a hoarse voice! We therefore urge extreme caution before you do anything about changing your pitch level. Make sure that you have followed the routine of determining optimum pitch as outlined in Chapter 3, and do not trust to your own unaided judgment.

When working on interval, inflection, intonation, emphasis, phrasing, and flexibility, it will be advantageous to study parts of your recorded speeches phrase by phrase. This can be done by stopping the tape at the pauses. Thus you will know at once whether your phrasing follows the units of thought, whether you are hesitating instead of pausing (non-fluency), and whether your emphasis is misplaced. Of course, you cannot diagnose all the factors at one listening; you will replay the same phrases again and again.

When listening for factors relating to range, you may even want to work at the piano. Locating your highest comfortable pitch in a phrase and your lowest, hum them in turn until you have identified them on the piano. Thus you will be able to get a fairly exact graph of your interval or range. Inflection and intonation are more subjective elements and will have to be judged somewhat intuitively, but even with these it is easier to make an analysis if the study is made phrase by phrase.

Lest you begin to think that a diagnosis of your own voice is too complex for you to undertake, let us hasten to reassure you. Almost anyone can train his ear to hear the voice variables; and while no one can hear a score of factors simultaneously, almost anyone can hear them one at a time by using selective attention.

6. List your voice problems.

a. Put the most difficult first, the easiest last. In general we may say that the most stubborn problems are found in points 1 and 2 of the Voice Rating Sheet—"Pitch" and "Quality." For example, if you have a voice showing hoarseness or harshness, you should probably start at that point rather than, let us say, with "Loudness."

b. Sometimes the factors will cluster. For example, "Phrasing" will usually go with "Fluency" and with "Emphasis." In such a case an attack upon the central problem will tend to bring help all down the line. The key is to get away from reading or reciting and begin talking to people as individuals. Ministerial tune, to take another example, will show itself in the distortion of a number of factors including "Inflection," "Intonation," and "Flexibility," as well as under pathos and melism. The attack upon any one of these factors will therefore be most effective when the root cause is known and worked upon. A Chart of Typical Speech Problems beginning on p. 136 deals with some of the most usual clustering.

7. Isolate your problems and work on one at a time. Observing the principle of clustering just mentioned, you will do well to group your problems and work on one group at a time. Sometimes success in one area will bring relief in another, but this will be a by-product of selective attention to the most pressing needs at the time. Problems of "Quality" are very different from those of "Rate," although "Loudness" may be contributing to "Harshness." The best way of working at each problem will be found in using the index.

8. Practice until you have made improvements automatic. There is no escaping vocal exercises. These must be repeated until they become second nature. The reason is that no speaker dares to be thinking about the voice variables while he is delivering a speech, any more than an automobile driver should be thinking about brake and clutch and accelerator while driving down the street. No driver is a good driver while these mechanical matters are still in the foreground of his attention. The cure? Take driving lessons

until these necessary actions become automatic! Practice the voice variables until they have been mastered! You must drill until you have made good speech second nature.

Like the little boy trying to escape his piano lessons, we may want to skip practice, but there can be no improvement without it.

Practice daily. A breathing exercise done for five minutes three times a day will do more good than the same exercise repeated for three continuous hours on Saturday.

9. Incorporate your improvements into daily conversational talk. The best testing ground for your new communication skill will not be found on the public platform but at the dining table, in the living room, and at informal gatherings where you are merely conversing. A man's speech, formal and informal, roots in one system. Many ministers become self-conscious in the pulpit because they are admittedly careless in daily conversation. Informal talk offers the easiest and most natural place for self-correction. A man does not usually feel as free to correct himself in the pulpit as he does during friendly conversation. This is especially true of mistakes in articulation and pronunciation. But it need be no less true of any of the voice variables. A man who has been talking without proper breath control, for instance, should put his new breathing techniques to work every day in everything he says from "Hello" to "Good-by."

10. Test and consolidate the integration of your speaking skills by reading the Bible aloud every day. Good oral reading is like good talking, and the mastery of public reading leads to great improvement in public speaking. For the purpose of practice, oral reading has one immense advantage over speaking. It liberates the mind from formulating thoughts into words and permits the focusing of attention upon the expression of thoughts. Thus you may read to practice proper breathing and pausing, or good interval, or effective emphasis; then you can move on from isolated exercises to an integration of all factors until your reading is as clear and forceful as possible.

11. Separate practice from your public speaking. The speaking situation is such that you will do your best only when your mind is

intent upon sharing a message with your hearers. This involves the pressure of an idea worth sharing, an intense desire to share, a vivid grasp of the ideas as they are being shared, together with a two-way visual-pantomimic-vocal communication between you and the people who sit before you. Obviously, if your conscious mind is busy with this task, there will be no time to think about the voice variables. If you do begin to think about them, your speech will disintegrate for want of a vital core.

We are not suggesting that you should be able to exclude completely criticism from delivery. In spite of everything, you will be painfully self-conscious for a while and you may even regress momentarily; but after a little fumbling you should be able to make the transition with reasonable comfort. Meantime, get something to say that you feel deeply about and tell it to your people with all your heart, make it real and make it personal—not necessarily profound or beautiful, just genuine and helpful to people.

A man of our acquaintance has a very simple cure for self-consciousness: "Just lean up hard against the purpose of your speech." This is an excellent suggestion; to it more can be added. Boil the ideas down to one sentence and say it to yourself just before you begin. And look at your hearers as individuals, one by one. If you are sitting during the service where you can look unobtrusively at your congregation, form the habit of seeing them individual by individual, rather than as a mass.

This preliminary exercise with purpose, theme, and people will help to focus your mind where it belongs and enable you to do your best. Meantime, gains from practice will slowly be incorporating themselves into your public speaking.

12. Remember that along with your sermon you deliver yourself. A man speaks with his body as well as with his words, with his feelings as well as with his ideas. On the one hand, the visual impression conveyed by the action of the speaker may ratify or veto his words; in an effective speech the message that is heard must be underscored and emphasized pantomimically by the message that is seen. On the other hand, the participation of the body in delivery is far deeper and more intimate than any visual impression. The

nature and degree of a speaker's physical participation will show up in his voice; it will be heard as well as seen. Tone color in a voice, or changing resonance, reflects feelings; but the feelings themselves, to be genuine, must be experienced physiologically. Each deeply felt emotion has its own proper set of muscle tensions through the whole organism. Therefore, the emotional honesty of a voice will depend upon a speaker's ability to communicate his message with his whole body. (See Chapters 6 and 7.)

The bonds between a man's public speech and his private personality are indissoluble. Many of the problems of speech cannot be solved without a change in personality. The change need not be a revolution in all cases; sometimes it can be a liberation. There is no man who will not be a better public speaker if he comes to know himself better. And no one can do this alone, by introspection. Many men try to do it alone, but we have never known one who succeeded.

It may ultimately become accepted practice for everyone entering the ministry to participate in personal counseling sessions with a trained counselor until a minimum of self-insight is achieved. The notion that every man who seeks the services of a counselor is neurotic or abnormal unfortunately does exist. How much better to think of counseling in terms of the priesthood of believers— which means not that each man is his own priest before God but that we are priests to each other, I to you and you to me. We need each other. In biblical terms, this means that where two men are met together in complete candor and mutual acceptance a Third Person is present, and that Person is found as a Redeemer (Matthew 18:20). Or, to say it differently, in a genuine counseling situation the interpersonal relationship envelops those who accept each other; it makes of them, together, something more than they are as a simple sum of two individuals. It is not amiss to say that the togetherness cannot be made, but that it grows—that it is organismic or near-organismic—and that it overcomes isolation and solitariness. In a sense, it creates a new family, into which an immature person can be reborn and within which he can grow toward emotional maturity. A Christian is not afraid to say that the togetherness is more than human, that it is cosmic, and that it is a part of the life of God in the midst of His people.

It is in such an atmosphere that harsh realities are faced and accepted, that unrealized capacities come to light—that insight is achieved, forgiveness experienced, and character changed. Do ministers dare to urge this upon others without experiencing it themselves?

There are deeper reasons for seeking a personal counselor than to become a more effective speaker, of course; but we are saying here that many problems of speech will refuse to yield until they are carried back into the inner citadel of personality from which they emerged.

You have set out upon a big undertaking. Do not sell it short. And do not be discouraged if you do not get speedy and spectacular results. You grew into your present speaking habits over a number of years. You cannot be expected to outgrow them in a few days or weeks. Decide right now that you will give the project at least ten months or a year. And keep at it persistently day by day. If you will do this, we are certain that you will come out at the end a greatly improved speaker.

Appendices

APPENDIX A: RATING SHEETS

VOICE RATING SHEET

	Very Good	Good	Average	Poor	Very Poor		
1. Pitch							
a. Pitch level (Over-all)	( )	( )	( )	( )	( )		
b. Range (Interval)	( )	( )	( )	( )	( )		
c. Intonation (melody pattern)	( )	( )	( )	( )	( )		
d. Inflection	( )	( )	( )	( )	( )		
2 Quality							
a. Freedom from breathiness	( )	( )	( )	( )	( )		
b. Freedom from nasality	( )	( )	( )	( )	( )	Hyper Hypo	( ) ( )
c. Freedom from harshness	( )	( )	( )	( )	( )		
d. Freedom from hoarseness	( )	( )	( )	( )	( )		
3. Articulation	( )	( )	( )	( )	( )	Regional Foreign	( ) ( )
4. Pronunciation	( )	( )	( )	( )	( )		
5. Rate							
a. Over-all	( )	( )	( )	( )	( )	Fast Slow	( ) ( )
b. Flexibility	( )	( )	( )	( )	( )		
c. Fluency	( )	( )	( )	( )	( )		
6. Loudness							
a. Over-all	( )	( )	( )	( )	( )	Loud Soft	( ) ( )
b. Emphasis	( )	( )	( )	( )	( )		
7. Phrasing	( )	( )	( )	( )	( )		

BODY RATING SHEET

	Very Good	Good	Average	Poor	Very Poor		
1. Posture							
a. During approach	( )	( )	( )	( )	( )		
b. During delivery	( )	( )	( )	( )	( )		
2. Physical Activity							
a. Gestures	( )	( )	( )	( )	( )	Mannerisms	( )
b. Change of position	( )	( )	( )	( )	( )	Mannerisms	( )
c. Use of notes	( )	( )	( )	( )	( )		
d. Facial expression	( )	( )	( )	( )	( )	Mannerisms	( )
e. Eye contact	( )	( )	( )	( )	( )		

The rating sheet facing this page should be used with caution. The semantic value of terms will necessarily vary somewhat from person to person scoring the sheet. Therefore, it is the total clustering of scores on each sheet that should be used in reaching a conclusion. There are numerous emotions which could not be listed in so brief a space; users should feel free to add others in the spaces provided. In no case should the rating sheet be made a substitute for intuitive judgment expressed in one's own words. And in every case the results of the scoring should be discussed with one or more fellow listeners. The effort to capture feelings in a net of words will probably always involve a good deal of trial and error, but experience has shown that a class can nearly always reach a high degree of unanimity through discussion.

RATING SHEET OF EMOTIONS

	Yes	Some	No	Un-decided
I. Melism (immediate feelings)				
1. Audience rapport	( )	( )	( )	( )
2. Creativity	( )	( )	( )	( )
3. Preparedness	( )	( )	( )	( )
4. Self-confidence	( )	( )	( )	( )
5. Will to communicate	( )	( )	( )	( )
II. Pathos (deep, persistent feelings)				
1. Apathy	( )	( )	( )	( )
2. Apology	( )	( )	( )	( )
3. Constriction (fearfulness)	( )	( )	( )	( )
4. Conviction	( )	( )	( )	( )
5. Defensiveness	( )	( )	( )	( )
6. Desire to punish	( )	( )	( )	( )
7. Excessive meekness	( )	( )	( )	( )
8. Excessive righteousness	( )	( )	( )	( )
9. Fellow-feeling	( )	( )	( )	( )
10. Hostility	( )	( )	( )	( )
11. Over-dramatization	( )	( )	( )	( )
12. Pedantry	( )	( )	( )	( )
13. Pontification	( )	( )	( )	( )
14. Pugnacity	( )	( )	( )	( )
15. Security	( )	( )	( )	( )
16. Self-acceptance	( )	( )	( )	( )
17. Self-consciousness	( )	( )	( )	( )
18. Sense of humor	( )	( )	( )	( )
19. Sincerity	( )	( )	( )	( )
20. Others:	( )	( )	( )	( )

APPENDIX B:

A CHART OF TYPICAL SPEECH PROBLEMS

Monotony of Pitch (Monotone)
A. Description: Little or no inflection or interval; melody almost lacking
B. Possible Causes
   1. Organic: Hearing loss.
   2. Functional.
      a. Lack of awareness of voice variables.
      b. Defensiveness in personality of speaker.
      c. Imitation of stereotype.
      d. Stage fright.
      e. Talking at rather than to people.
C. Therapy
   1. Ear training. See Chapter 2, pp. 11-15.
   2. Developing a conversational tone. See Chapter 5, pp. 58-59.
   3. Relaxation. See Appendix C, pp. 144-145.

Unrelieved High Pitch
A. Description: Voice tends to be shrill, penetrating.
B. Possible causes
   1. Pitch tends to rise as volume increases.
   2. Excitement; nervous tension.
C. Therapy
   1. Before coming into the pulpit practice the progressive relaxation exercises. See Appendix C, pp. 144-145.
   2. Anchor yourself well at the beginning of the speech. Begin conversationally at your own optimum pitch. See p. 20.
   3. If during the speech you catch yourself rising to a shrill pitch, deliberately pull it down to normal. (Be careful not to overcompensate by straining it too low.)
   4. Speak directly to people as individuals. See Chapter 5, pp. 58-59.

Ministerial Tune (See Chapter 5.)

Hoarseness
A. Description: Strained vocal cords.
   1. Chronic hoarseness—like a perpetual cold in the throat.
   2. Spasmodic hoarseness, following a public speech, or during a speech, or possibly only in its latter stages.

B. Possible causes, functional
  1. Of chronic hoarseness.
     a. Habitually speaking at a pitch level below one's optimum pitch—straining for a deep bass voice.
     b. Wrong breathing—speaking from the throat muscles rather than from the diaphragm.
  2. Of spasmodic hoarseness.
     a. A tense throat—excessive nervousness, and/or
     b. Public speaking at a high pitch level—excited, shrill speech, or
     c. Public speaking at a low pitch level—not a regular speaking habit, but one employed only in *public* speech.
C. Possible causes, organic
  1. Allergies.
  2. Post-nasal drip.
  3. Nodules.
  4. Contact ulcer.
  5. Paralyzed vocal cord.
D. Therapy
  1. Check with your physician to make sure there is no organic involvement.
  2. Determine and drill upon your optimum pitch. See Chapter 3, p. 20.
  3. Practice breathing and speaking from the diaphragm. See Chapter 4 and Appendix C.
  4. Practice progressive relaxation, aiming at a relaxed and open throat. See Chapter 3 and Appendix C, pp. 144-145.

Breathiness
A. Description
  1. Quality disorder: too much air seems to be escaping through vocal cords.
  2. Voice sounds weak, childish, or tired.
B. Possible causes
  1. Improper use of vocal machine. Not enough energy provided.
  2. Infantile personality.
  3. Stage fright.
C. Therapy
  1. Breathing exercises. See Appendix C, pp. 145-146.
  2. Relaxation. See Appendix C, pp. 144-145.
  3. Personality insight. See Chapter 7.

Harshness

A. Description
   1. Voice quality deviation: quality is sharp and coarse; has little mellowness.
   2. Sounds intense, aggressive, or officious.

B. Possible causes
   1. Excessive tension; oral cavity surfaces are tight and reflect sounds sharply.
   2. Personality disposition: overly dominant nature, overly aggressive, occasionally hostile.
   3. Improper effort toward projecting the voice. Push is made from throat muscles rather than diaphragm.

C. Therapy
   1. Ear training to become aware of voice quality differences. See Chapter 2.
   2. Personality re-evaluation. See Chapter 7.
   3. Breathing re-education. See Appendix C, pp. 145-146.
   4. Resonance exercises. See Appendix C, pp. 146-147.

Nasality (hyper)

A. Description
   1. Voice seems to be coming unduly or entirely from the nose.
   2. Sharp, unpleasant nasal quality; little oral quality.

B. Possible causes
   1. Organic.
      a. Cleft palate.
      b. Paralyzed soft palate.
   2. Functional.
      a. Lack of awareness of voice quality.
      b. Regionalism. In the Midwest, Northeast, and some parts of the South, the tendency is to nasalize vowels excessively.
      c. After tonsillectomy, if tonsils were greatly enlarged and person has been using them to assist in making closure between oral and nasal cavities, there will be a tendency toward nasal speech until new adjustment has been made.

C. Therapy
   1. Surgery or prosthesis for cleft palate.
   2. Ear training to become aware of quality differences. See Chapter 2.
   3. Practice in vocalizing using oral quality.

4. Exercises to activate the soft palate. Blowing bits of paper across a table; blowing out candles, etc.

Nasality (hypo)

A. Description: Lack of nasal resonation. Nasal passages seem to be blocked. "Cold-in-the-head" sound; muffled, thick quality.

B. Possible causes
1. Organic.
   a. Any obstruction or deviation in the nasal passages or those leading to them.
   b. Chronic sinusitis, enlarged tonsils or adenoids, etc., are common causes.
2. Functional: comparatively rare.

C. Therapy: Medical attention to evaluate and/or eliminate deviation.

Lazy Articulation (See Chapter 3, pp. 28-35, and Appendix C, p. 152.

Sigmatism

A. Description: A type of articulation disorder that applies only to the production of the "*s*" sound.
1. The *s* is whistled, or is produced with too much escape of air so that it has a hissing sound.
2. Lateral lisp. The *s* is produced with the sides of the tongue too relaxed so that the air escapes over the sides rather than the tip of the tongue. The result is a mushy sound. *Yes* will sound like *Yesh*.

B. Possible causes
1. Poor sound discrimination.
2. Possibly a slight hearing loss for high-frequency sounds (the *s* is high frequency).
3. Dental anomalies.
4. Inadequate dentures.
5. Imitation.
6. Habit.

C. Therapy
1. If you have any suspicion that you might have a hearing loss, have your hearing evaluated.
2. If you wear dentures, check with your dentist for better fit.
3. Get practice in learning to hear the sound produced correctly and incorrectly.
4. Hold the sides of the tongue tightly against the roof of the

mouth when saying *s*. Let the air escape only through a narrow opening where the tonguetip is almost touching the upper or lower teeth. (The sound may be produced with tonguetip behind either upper or lower teeth. Select position which seems most natural for you.) If your own efforts or those of your friends are ineffective, consult a certified speech therapist.

Monotony of Rate

A. Description: Phrases and words spoken too much alike; no change of pace.

B. Possible causes: Much like those of ministerial tune.

C. Therapy
   1. The same as for ministerial tune.
   2. Also reread Chapter 8 on "Reading the Bible Aloud."
   3. Develop flexibility in staccato and legato phonation. See Appendix C, pp. 153-154.

Hesitant, Lurching Delivery

A. Description
   1. Misplaced pauses, poor phrasing, and/or
   2. Verbalized pauses—*ah, uh.*

B. Possible causes: Many, including one or more of the following:
   1. Reciting or reading the speech instead of re-creating it at the moment of delivery.
   2. Dropping a phrase from the mind when it is only half-finished, to go on mentally to the phrase next to be spoken.
   3. Fear of silences, or ignorance of the important role of silence through adequate pauses. (Allowing absolutely no "dead air.")
   4. Staccato phonation: syllables spoken so rapidly that the tongue races ahead of the brain. See Appendix C, pp. 153-154.

C. Therapy
   1. For verbalized pauses: enlist the aid of a tape recorder and a friend. Become painfully aware of them.
   2. For staccato phonation; see exercises in Appendix C.
   3. Cultivate the art of meaningful pauses. Learn to trust and use silences. See pp. 38-39.
   4. Finish thoughts and phrases together; use the pause to think ahead to the next phrase. (The mind moves forward, not as a steady continuum, but by alternate leaps and focusings. Teach your mind to leap during the pauses, rather than during the phrases.)

Extremes of Loudness

A. Description: This fault takes various forms:
   1. Both extremes may exist together, the speaker now shouting and then whispering—like a cliff jumper.
   2. Habitual shouting through the whole speech.
   3. Spasmodic whispering, for special emphasis.
   4. Spasmodic shouting for special emphasis.
B. Possible causes: An abortive attempt to gain emphasis or to be heard.
C. Therapy: Employ proper modes of emphasis
   1. Use controlled intensity for the material to be emphasized, i.e., increase the rhythm—accent more words in the most important phrases. (The effect will be that of power held in reserve.)
   2. Slow down the rate in pronouncing both important individual words and key phrases.
   3. Emphasize selectively only those ideas that are truly climactic; then they will stand out by contrast.
   4. Let your breath do the work to achieve adequate loudness, not your throat.
   5. Talk *to* your audience, not at or over it.

Poor Eye Contact

A. Description
   1. Speaker may be tied to notes or manuscript, and/or
   2. Speaker looks away from his auditors, at the floor or wall, or out the window.
B. Possible causes
   1. Bad training; i.e., some misinformed teachers of speech have advised their pupils not to look at their auditors, lest they be distracted by the sight!
   2. Inadequate preparation.
   3. Fear of the audience.
C. Therapy
   1. Master those notes, or dispense with them entirely.
   2. Do not think of your audience as a crowd but as a gathering of individuals.
      a. Make yourself look at several of them as individuals before you begin speaking.
      b. Select given individuals in various parts of the audience and talk directly to them.

c. Make it a point to observe their facial expressions, their wearing apparel, and, if you are close enough, even the color of their eyes.

Mannerisms

I. Rhythmic swaying of body; teetering up and down on toes.

A. Description: Automatic biological rhythms.

B. Possible causes: Much like that behind ministerial tune—a division between thought and emotion.

C. Therapy

1. Direct: Since they are largely unconscious actions, get a friend to note and inform you of them.

2. Basic: Train your perceptual imagination so that you will learn to deliver the speech with your whole body. See Chapter 6 and Appendix C.

II. Nervous hands and feet; random activities which distract attention.

A. Description: As above.

B. Possible cause: Excessive nervousness.

C. Therapy

1. Direct attention through the courtesy of a friend.

2. Practice the relaxation exercises, Appendix C.

III. Compulsive, stereotyped gestures.

A. Description: Any gesture which is used so frequently that it draws attention to itself (i.e., pulling the lobe of the ear, brushing back one's hair, buttoning and unbuttoning one's coat, pointing the finger at the audience).

B. Possible cause: Probably mildly neurotic, but nearly all speakers develop such gestures.

C. Therapy: Get a friend to spot them and break them up before they are deeply entrenched. Warning: You will keep forming new ones to replace the old ones; eternal vigilance is the price of freedom.

IV. Nervous clearing of throat, excessive use of certain words or phrases; stereotyped inflection, melody, rhythm.

A. Description: Any vocal or language characteristic that is so habitual that it calls attention to itself—"ah," "my friends."

B. Possible Causes

1. Nervousness.

2. Poor training in listening to oneself.

3. Lack of preparation.

4. Limited vocabulary.
5. Misdirected pathos.

C. Therapy
   1. Find out what it is you are afraid of.
   2. Get a friend to check you for voice or language mannerisms and then work toward eliminating those discovered.
   3. Develop a conversational style.

APPENDIX C: EXERCISES

I. Relaxation

1. Lie on the floor on your back. Extend your right arm from your shoulder, raising it about four inches from the floor. Extend the fingers and tense every muscle in the arm and hand until the arm trembles and the tension is almost painful. Now systematically "let go," first with the fingers while maintaining an awareness of the remaining tension in the hand and arm, next at the wrist while keeping the arm tense. Finally, "let go" from the shoulders.

2. Tense the right arm as previously, and then the left. Both arms will then be extended in a tense position with the hands about four inches from the floor. "Let go" systematically with the right arm and then with the left. Then try "letting go" with both together.

3. Lift the right foot about one inch from the floor, point the toes and tense the whole leg and foot until the muscles tremble. Then add the left leg in the same manner. "Let go" systematically, beginning at the toes of each foot in turn.

4. Keeping arms and legs tense, bring the throat and shoulders into a tense condition. Draw the chin down rigidly toward the chest and in against the neck; pull the shoulders in toward the neck. Then "let go" with various muscle groups one at a time until all have been relaxed.

5. Attain the generally tense condition for the entire body, "letting go" of one muscle group at a time in the following order: fingers, wrist, lower arm, upper arm; repeat for the second arm; toes, ankles, knee, hip; repeat for the other leg; shoulder, chin, neck, and throat. Lie limp and heavy.

6. Utter *ah* as in a deep sigh.

7. Repeat the above exercises sitting in a chair, arms extended horizontally at the sides and feet lifted a few inches from the floor. As the arms are relaxed, let gravity drop them at the side, etc.

8. Let your head drop forward toward your chest, then slowly roll it over the left shoulder, and drop into its initial position. Be sure that the jaw muscles are completely relaxed throughout this exercise, and as nearly as possible let the head fall around its orbit by its own weight.

9. Vocalize the *ah* sound and repeat, gradually eliminating any excessive breathiness until you achieve a clear, easy tone. Repeat with several vowel sounds and groups of sounds, i.e., *ha, he, high, ho, how,*

hoi, etc. Now, with relaxed throat but without breathiness, speak a short sentence. Let the tones float out, soft and clear.

10. Stand erect and repeat exercises 1-6 as nearly as a standing position will allow. Then repeat exercise 9.

II. Posture

Objective: A responsive body, proper gesture.

1. After the relaxation exercises, stand easily erect.

2. Imagine that you are supported by an invisible wire from the ceiling attached to your chest, but the wire is not so tight that it throws you into a military brace. In other words, stand tall; avoid stooping, slumping, or sagging on one foot.

3. The head should be up and at ease. Harmful variations: chin on chest, eyes looking over one's spectacles; chin drawn back, neck muscles straining.

4. Hands and arms relaxed and ready for various gestures. Not locked behind the back, nor on the pulpit, nor held rigidly at one's side.

5. Do not worry about your feet. If you are standing tall, they will take care of themselves.

III. Breathing

Objective: An adequate air supply for the production of clear tone without throat constriction.

1. Stand tall before a mirror. With fingertips together, place the palms of your hands across your abdomen just above the belt line. Begin to watch your breathing action. If the shoulders rise and fall you are probably breathing inefficiently for speech. Practice until the shoulders remain inactive and only the hands over the diaphragm move in and out. Inhale and exhale evenly.

2. Lie on the floor. Place a book on your diaphragm and let it ride easily up and down as you breathe. Do not consciously manipulate the muscles of the diaphragm; rather let the air push it out like a drum and then let the air escape as from a balloon.

3. Still lying on the floor, inhale normally, hold the breath an instant, then say *how.* Repeat several times.

4. Remain prone. Inhale quickly through the mouth, yet easily and without gasping; take a full breath. With controlled exhalation, trying to save breath, say *how, how, how, how, how.* Repeat using *ha, high,*

he, ho, hoi, etc. Inhalation should be quick; exhalation slow and controlled.

5. Remain prone. Inhale quickly and easily; then count as high as you can go without strain. Inhale again and repeat, endeavoring to conserve breath on each number so as to count higher at each endeavor.

6. Stand erect and repeat exercises 3, 4, and 5.

7. Using the same breathing action, connect words into short sentences like: "One by one they took their places." Then add: "One by one and two by two they took their places," etc.

8. Take a passage of scripture or a poem and mark a stroke (/) at the end of each phrase. Read the phrases, first taking a quick, deep breath. Pause at each stroke to take a breath. At minor pauses merely replenish lost breath; but at major pauses exhale and then quickly and easily inhale, and continue reading. Do not speak until you run out of air; keep a full tank of air by inhaling at each pause. In the early stages of such reading, place one hand over the diaphragm. If possible, have someone watch to make sure that you are not moving your shoulders.

9. After the correct breathing habits are fairly well established, practice out-loud reading for a few minutes each day, concentrating on quick, easy inhalation, sustaining the breath through each phrase, and replenishing it at each pause.

IV. Resonance

Objective: A clear, undistorted tone, resonated in a relaxed, open throat and mouth and easily projected to the listener.

1. As a preparation for the exercise in resonance, do the exercises in progressive relaxation. Or, as an absolutely minimum preparation, do the following:

a. Bend the body forward from the waist, letting the arms swing freely and the torso sag of its own weight. Let go. Slowly rise and stand relaxed.

b. Drop the chin toward the chest and let your head hang. Now slowly, to the count of ten, with the jaw completely relaxed like a dead hinge, let the head pivot on the neck in a complete 360-degree roll. Slowly! Make the neck muscles as limp as possible during this exercise; let the head seem to fall around the pivot.

2. Assume normal speaking posture, still relaxed.

3. With the tongue resting on the floor of the mouth, sigh, vocalizing the *ah* sound.

4. Let the *ah* sigh expand naturally into a yawn.

5. Now, with the throat relaxed and open, and with easy tone, chant a part of a psalm or other scripture.

6. Verse by verse, alternately chanting and reading scripture, letting the throat remain open and relaxed. Let the tone be easy and effortless, but without breathiness.

7. Experiment with the placement of tones, using the principal vowel and diphthong sounds preceded by the *h* sound, i.e., *ha, ho, he, hi, hoo, hoi*, etc. Produce each sound in two ways, first confining it to the back of the throat and then placing it in imagination on a definite spot about five feet in front of your mouth. Repeat with each sound.

8. Stand in a large room or auditorium and repeat exercises 5, 6, and 7 while projecting to the back row of seats. Do not force the tone from the throat, but let it float out.

V. Nasal Resonance

Objective: The overcoming of hyper-nasality; a pleasant, well-resonated tone.

1. In turn say the consonants *m* (as in *mine*), *n* (as in *no*), and *ng* (as in *sing*), sustaining each sound as a short hum. These three are the only sounds in English speech which are exclusively resonated in the nasal cavities. As you hum each sound, place your fingers on the bony part of the nose; you should feel the vibrations and become aware of the sounds being emitted through the nose rather than the mouth.

2. Next, start with *m* and then vocalize *o* (as in *old*). Continue, using other vowel sounds in combination first with *m* and then with *n* as in *mo, me, my, may, no, ne, nigh, nay*. See if these vowels are vibrating in your nose and head; if so you are excessively nasal.

3. To further sharpen your ear, practice moving from oral sounds to nasal sounds as in *ohm, aim, I'm, him, and, an, in, own*. Note this time that you should be moving from an oral tone to a nasal tone.

4. Now practice moving from nasal sounds to oral and back to nasal, as in *mine, mean, moon, moan, main, men, man, ming*.

5. Try these words and see if your ear or your sense of vibrations can tell where the resonation normally belongs (remembering that only *m, n*, and *ng* should be nasal): *mango, singing, morning, mingling, monsoon, psalm, Solomon, salvation, benediction*.

6. The following quotations from the Bible are so arranged that a line completely free of nasal consonants is followed by a line containing nasal consonants. See if you can differentiate between, and read the

lines without nasal consonants so that nasal sounds are greatly minimized, if not completely eliminated:

> For the ear trieth words, as the palate tasteth food.
> Therefore, hearken unto me, ye men of understanding.
> Let us choose for us that which is right.
> Man that is in honor and understandeth not.
> Is like the beast that perisheth.
> It was morning and it was evening one day.
> Ye daughters of Israel, weep over Saul.
> How are the mighty fallen in the midst of the battle.
> Wherefore should I fear at the days of evil,
> When iniquity at my heels compasseth me about?
> They that trust to their wealth
> And boast themselves in the multitude of their riches . . .
> This their way is their folly.
> Yet after them men approve their saying.
> Death shall be their shepherd,
> And the upright shall have dominion over them in the morning.

VI.   Perceptual Creativity

A. To Develop Visual Creativity

1. Walk to the nearest window looking out to the street and for
about twenty seconds examine generally all the things that are visible.

2. Now that you have taken in the total scene begin watching systematically. First, focus all your attention on the colors in the scene.
Note the color of the bare earth, the barren trees and bushes. Observe
the sky. Is it a Wedgwood blue, or is it lighter or darker? Are the
clouds snowy white or tinged with gray or purple? Explore the houses
or buildings across the street. Are they red brick trimmed in white frame
or are they wooden, painted yellow with chocolate-brown shutters? Are
people passing? If so, notice their clothing. Is the lady's coat maroon
or bright red? Notice the feather in her hat. Is it white or gray?

Keep watching in this manner until you have exhausted all the
possibilities.

3. Next, examine closely the shapes and lines in the scene. Note
the architecture of all the structures. Do the roofs slant or are they
flat? Observe the tree lines and the shrubbery. Are they planned or
do they seem unrelated to the structures? Do the wires strung from
pole to pole make interesting or monotonous patterns?

4. Note next the texture of what you see. Do the houses seem flimsy and light, capable of being blown away; or do they appear rocklike, sturdy enough to withstand the severest storm? Observe the grass again. Does it seem velvety-thick or is it thin and sparse?

5. Having done these things return to your chair and try to recall all of what you have visually observed. Describe aloud, but not necessarily in correct grammatical form or with animation, all that you recall. Remember to include color, line, and texture.

6. Now that you have formulated most of the words, imagine that you are describing it to an interested friend. This time use normal sentence structure and animation.

Observe as you talk how your body automatically responds as you describe the scene. Your hands will occasionally seem to perform without conscious direction as they move to show shape or line. Your face may light up with a smile as you describe a flowering magnolia bush or a shaggy brown dog. Note also how your entire body quite effortlessly and naturally helps to describe the scene. Nothing should seem contrived or mechanical; self-consciousness is minimized as your attention is completely directed toward describing what you saw.

7. Your next step, taken from memory, is to recall a scene or a setting very familiar to you—your living room, your office, or your garden early in June. Then using the same procedures just described, bring into words and then into conversation its visual details—color, line, texture. You may have some initial difficulty with this. Although you have selected for recall a room where you have been hundreds of times, you may discover to your dismay that you have no clear concept whatsoever of the visual details of that room. If forced to describe it you would probably say, "Well, it's just an ordinary room, much like any other room." Of course, when you go and actually examine that room in the manner we have been describing, you will find that it is very different from other rooms. You may have to spend some time merely reexamining familiar scenes before you can perform this exercise with any degree of success.

8. Finally, imagine yourself in a situation or setting in which you have never been except vicariously through written or oral accounts. Use the same techniques you performed earlier, but this time first let your imagination build in the basic units (buildings, landscape, etc.). With basic units structured, proceed to analyze details, formulate words, and finally to describe to an imaginary friend or audience what

you have seen. *Note:* There is only one danger in this process. Be certain you have at least a general idea of the real setting or object you are describing. If you are not sure, use an encyclopedia. It would be ludicrous to have velvety green grass growing near the peak of Mount Everest!

B. To Develop Auditory Creativity

1. Stand at the same window we described previously; open it if the weather permits. Try to keep the visual impressions from coming clearly into focus; close your eyes if it helps; give your full attention to listening to all the sounds.

2. Begin listening more systematically. Concentrate first on all machine noises: automobiles, lawn mowers, distant airplanes or trains. Next, shift your attention to all the sounds of nature: chirps and twitters of birds, the creaking of branches, the rustling of leaves. Listen then to the human noises: muffled voices, children's shrieks, footsteps, laughter. As you listen, you may hear the town clock striking or the shrill scream of the police or fire siren.

3. Keep listening until you have exhausted all possibilities. Then proceed in the same manner as in steps 5, 6, 7, and 8 described previously, remembering to change your descriptions to what you have *heard*.

You may find it interesting to observe your bodily tensions both while you are listening and while you are recalling and describing. Your muscles will take on a degree of expectant tension as you discover that it is almost impossible to listen intently without remaining perfectly quiet yourself. As you recall and describe, this same muscle tension reappears. Just as in visual recall your body again tells its own story.

C. To Develop Tactile Creativity

1. Take any common object like your pencil. Hold it in your hands and to black out temporarily the visual impressions close your eyes. Examine the object carefully with your fingers. Check its demensions, then estimate its weight. What material does it seem to be made of? Is it metal or wood, ivory or gold, rough or smooth? How about the workmanship? Do the parts fit snugly together or are there gaps?

2. Keep examining the object with your fingers until you have exhausted the possibilities. Then proceed with steps 5, 6, 7, and 8

described in Unit A, remembering to change your descriptions to what you have *touched*.

D. To Develop Olfactory Creativity

Stand at the same window we have been referring to, only this time the window should be open and the month is May. The air is full of scents. Direct all your attention to them. The crabapple tree which you can touch by extending your hand is in full bloom; its blossoms have a sweet fragrance. A climbing rosebush shows large buds. One or two roses are open right by the window's edge, and for some strange reason their odor reminds you of new-mown hay. Below the window you observe that the mint is growing and at the same time you catch a minty scent that reminds you of chewing gum and jelly. Your neighbor is watering his flower beds and you catch just a tinge of the dusty odor you always smell when the city department sprinkles the streets during the dry summer.

Keep sniffing and smelling and analyzing until you have exhausted all possibilities, then proceed in the same manner as in steps 5, 6, 7, and 8 in Unit A, remembering to change your descriptions to what you have *smelled*.

You will probably discover that it is comparatively difficult to find adequate words to describe the various odors. We can offer no remedy except to suggest some words that are available: *sweet, sour, stale, clean, fresh,* and the whole series of *like* words—*like new-mown hay, like fresh bread baking, like perfume,* etc.

Bodily activity will not be so marked in describing odors, but we can scarcely imagine anyone's describing the pungent odor of manure without wrinkling up his nose!

Yet one other major perception remains: *taste*. By this time it should be fairly clear how to proceed in becoming aware of the various senses and we will not reiterate. It should be pointed out, however, that taste is linked closely with smell and that the two frequently go hand in hand descriptively. The language again seems inadequate. Only a few words catch the full flavor: *bitter, sour, sweet, salty, spicy,* and *tasteless* are among the most popular.

E. To Develop Perceptual Versatility

It will be quite natural for one individual to tend to use one sensory percept more than another, and certainly this is far better than using none at all. However, it should be apparent that the more kinds of sensory perceptions that can be introduced into a sermon or speech the more alive it will become. A speaker must remember that although he may be almost exclusively a visually-oriented person many of his listeners may be auditory, and although they will appreciate his visual pictures they will "hear with him" when he uses auditory pictures. We suggest finally, therefore, that attention be given to all sensory factors. The results will be a living, stimulating message, believable to all listeners; freedom from excessive self-consiousness and fright; and a responsive body that reflects the ideas rather than gets in the way of them.

VII.   Flexibility of the Articulators

1. Purse the lips and, keeping them pursed, move them as far as possible in every direction.

2. Alternately draw the lips back and then purse them.

3. Project and point the tongue, keeping it in a horizontal plane.

4. Project and point the tongue and then touch the tip to the lower lip.

5. Project and point the tongue and then touch the tip to the upper lip.

6. Project and point the tongue and touch the tonguetip alternately to the upper and lower lips three times.

7. Project and point the tongue and then swing it slowly to the left, then back to the front and in.

8. Project and point the tongue and then swing it alternately to the left and right three times quite slowly, then in.

9. Project and point the tongue and then swing it slowly to the right, then back to the front and in.

10. Rotate the tonguetip slowly around the lips from left to right.

11. Rotate the tonguetip slowly around the lips from right to left.

12. Without sliding, touch the tonguetip successively to the center of the uper lip, to the left corner of the mouth, to the center of the lower lip, then to the right corner of the mouth. Repeat the exercise in reverse direction.

13. Slowly lift the tonguetip to the hard palate and then slowly relax it until it is flat in the mouth.

14. Starting at one end of the semicircle, with tonguetip touch in succession (with a sliding motion) the inside edges of the upper teeth,

then of the lower teeth. Repeat the exercise touching outside edges of the teeth.[1]

VIII. Articulation of Sounds

A. To Overcome Staccato Phonation

1. Phonate each of the following vowel sounds while counting silently and slowly to three:

    a. Long ē as in *see*. Repeat five times.
    b. Long ū as in *soon*. Repeat five times.
    c. *Aw* as in *all, saw*. Repeat five times.
    d. Broad ä as in *father*. Repeat five times.

2. Pronounce each of the following words, holding the long vowels for two counts (repeat several times):

eve	cool	dawn
eel	loop	taught
easy	tomb	sought
be	shoe	yawn
agree	voodoo	father
tree	room	ark
feet	soon	army
sleep	pool	heart
need	pursue	market

3. Pronounce the following pairs of words, making the first word in each pair excessively long but the second word clipped and short (repeat):

deep—dip	look—luck	sod—sad
feet—fit	cool—could	pop—put
deed—did	noon—none	psalm—sum
peak—pick	tooth—took	mop—map

4. Speak the following sentences, prolonging all the long vowels in the italicized words. Repeat several times, gradually approaching normal tempo but keeping the long vowels long:

    a. The *evenings* are *always cool because* of the *breeze* in the *trees*.
    b. *John argued ardently* about *honesty*.

[1] Adapted from Kirkpatrick, *The Creative Delivery of Sermons*, (Macmillan, 1947), pp. 206-208.

    c. *Paul's audience applauded warmly.*

    d. Though I *speak* with the tongues of men and of *angels* but have not *love* I am as *sounding brass* or a *tinkling cymbal.*

5. Choose any scripture passage and read it, emphasizing the important words and their weightier phrases by elongating the principal vowels in each emphatic word.

B. Correct Articulation of Troublesome Vowels and Diphthongs

1. Distinguishing ĕ (as in *dress*) from ĭ (as in *it*). Position: The three front vowels ē (as in *see*), ĭ (as in *it*), and ĕ (as in *dress*) are produced by placing the tongue on the floor of the mouth and arching it in front. The lips are open and relaxed. The first sound is emitted through teeth only slightly open; the second, with teeth a little farther open; and the third with teeth more open still.

a. Pronounce each three-word series, distinguishing each of the three vowel sounds. Repeat five times.

bead—bid—bed	deal—dill—dell
deep—dip—depth	peak—pick—peck
teen—tin—ten	feel—fill—fell

b. Pronounce the following pairs of words distinguishing clearly between the ĕ and ĭ sounds:

inside—ensign	since—cents
into—enter	impact—enact
insult—ensure	itch—etch

c. Read a brief passage from the Bible, recording your reading on tape. Play it back, listing all words in which the ĭ is substituted for ĕ. Repeat until all substitutions are eliminated.

2. The diphthong *au* as in *how*. This diphthong is produced by blending two vowel sounds, long ä (as in *father*) with short ŭ (as in *could*).

a. Begin by producing the two sounds separately: ä (*father*)— ŭ (*could*). Be sure the teeth are sufficiently wide apart for a good ä sound. Be careful not to substitute the front ă (as in *lack*). To make the ŭ sound, round and slightly pucker the lips.

b. Now combine the two sounds, shifting quickly from *ä* to *ŭ* until they become almost one sound. Be sure to articulate both sounds; do not drop the short *ŭ*.

c. Repeat the following words in series:

tot—toot—tout	don—dune—down
lot—loot—lout	ha—who—how
shot—shoot—shout	wad—wooed—wowed

d. Distinguish between the sounds in the following pairs of words:

pat—pout	spat—spout	tan—town
cad—cowed	mass—mouse	lad—loud
can't—count	bat—bout	bad—bowed
lot—lout	got—gout	dot—doubt
Scott—scout	shot—shout	trot—trout

e. Speak the following sentences, recording your reading and checking the result. Repeat until the diphthong in all cases is distinct.

We have found that this sound is a compound of vowels.

The mouth is usually rounded in shouting.

He plowed the ground around the house while his spouse spent an hour among the flowers.

3. The diphthong *ai* as in *ice*. This diphthong is produced by blending broad *ä* as in *father* with short *ĭ* as in *it*.

a. Begin by producing the two sounds separately. Then combine them. Do not substitute the flat *ă* as in *lack* for the broad *ä* as in *father*, nor drop the short *ĭ* sound.

b. Repeat the following words in series:

don—din—dine	pop—pip—pipe
top—tip—type	lock—lick—like
wan—win—wine	rod—rid—ride
hod—hid—hide	pock—pick—pike

c. Distinguish between sounds in the following pairs:

shod—shied	far—fire	wad—wide
wan—wine	mar—mire	tar—tire
sod—side	tot—tight	knot—night

d. Speak the following sentences into a tape recorder and repeat until the *ai* sound is clearly distinct in all cases.

My guide will buy me the right kind of line.

It would be wise to change the tire tonight.

Be kind to the crying child.

e. Check back over a recorded speech or reading for misarticulation of this diphthong. List all words containing a distortion or substitution for it. Practice these words. Then make a new recording of the same material. Repeat until all *ai* diphthongs are properly articulated.

4. The diphthong *oi* as in *boy*. This diphthong is produced by quickly blending the *aw* sound as in *all* with the short *ĭ* as in *it*. The most common fault in speaking this sound is to omit the *ĭ* sound.

a. Begin by voicing each sound separately. Then blend them. Be sure not to omit the short *ĭ*.

b. Repeat the following words in series:

call—kill—coil	tall—till—toil
maul—mill—moil	fall—fill—foil
ball—bill—boil	all—ill—oil

c. Distinguish between sounds in the following pairs:

ball—boil	lawn—loin	fall—foil
gnaws—noise	pause—poise	jaw—joy

d. Speak the following sentences into a tape recorder and repeat until the *oi* sound is clearly distinct from *aw*.

The shawl is in the automobile.

The point of the foil was poisoned.

The hawk caught the ball in his claw.

The boy was glad to hear his mother's voice.

Paul's audience applauded warmly.

He voiced his annoyance at the noise.

C. Distinguishing Between Words Used in Weaker and Stronger Forms

1. When not in an emphatic position, there are a number of words in English speech which are meant to be spoken in a weaker form. All these weaker forms are spoken quickly. A partial list of them follows:

a	could	him	should	us
am	does	his	some	was
an	for	into	such	we
and	from	me	than	were
are	had	must	that	where
as	has	nor	the	will
at	have	of	them	would
be	have to	or	there	you
but	he	shall	till	you are
can	her	she	to	your

2. The above words are made weaker in the following four ways, depending upon the word and whether neighboring sounds are vowels or consonants. The four changes are:

a. Changing to a weaker vowel, as in *the*, which moves from *thee* to *thuh*.
b. Dropping a vowel, as when *am* becomes *m*.
c. Dropping a consonant and weakening a vowel, as when *and* becomes *uhn*.
d. Dropping a consonant and a vowel, as when *and* becomes *n*, or *will* becomes *ll*.

3. Listen for these weaker forms in conversational speech.

4. Listen for violations of these weaker forms in the public reading and speaking of other men.

5. Listen for violations of them in your own recorded reading and speaking.

6. Read a passage of scripture, paying special attention to the speaking of unstressed words. Record and play back until all such words are subordinated.

D. Acquiring and Using the Phonetic Alphabet

The surest, and in the end the easiest, road to precise articulation is by way of the International Phonetic Alphabet. Anyone can master it and begin using it within a few days. The leisure time of a single week—fifteen to twenty minutes each day—should be entirely adequate. Once a person gets over the mistaken notion that phonetics is a foreign language and that the symbols are hard to learn, he has done the most difficult part of the task.

The reason for the phonetic alphabet is very simple. We have in written English a spelling alphabet of twenty-six letters; but in American speech we have about fifty sounds which all of us use every day. For the written or printed page the smaller alphabet is better, but for the spoken word it is not only inadequate; it is actually misleading. The double result is that many of us fail to hear speech as it really is and that, failing to hear, we also fail to articulate many of the sounds properly. When, on the other hand, we know all the symbols for all the sounds of spoken English we begin to hear more accurately and to speak more precisely.

In formulating the phonetic symbols, twenty-two of the letters of our regular English alphabet were used—all of them, in fact, except *c, q, x,* and *y.* So our task is already simplified; we do not have fifty symbols to learn, only twenty-eight. But wait! It is further simplified because nine of the sounds are diphthongs, each of which is made by combining the symbols of two vowels. Still further, the diphthongs have kinfolk among the consonantal sounds; these are the affricates, like the *t-sh* sound in *chocolate.* There are two affricates. So add nine diphthongs to two affricates and subtract the resultant eleven from the twenty-eight symbols to be learned; this leaves only seventeen symbols which are absolutely new, and they can be learned right now by anyone as he works his way on through this section:

We begin with the consonants. In each case we will give the phonetic symbol, a few key words in which the sound appears, and a brief direction for forming the sound in the mouth.

θ This is one of two *th* sounds. This particular one appears in words like *think, thousand,* and *breath.* It is spoken with the breath alone—in other words, as if whispered. To make this sound, simply place the tip of the tongue on the edge of the upper teeth and blow a gentle breath forcing tongue and teeth slightly apart.

ð This is the other *th* sound; it is spoken with the voice—not whispered—and is found in words like *the, this,* and *breathe.* To make this sound place the teeth as for θ and voice the sound as the tongue is vibrated against the teeth.

ʃ This symbol stands for *sh,* as in *show, wash, fishing.* It is an unvoiced breath blown over the tongue as the sides of the latter are touching the ridge at the base of the upper teeth, with the tip of the tongue free, though close to the upper teeth ridge and pointing slightly downward.

3 This is the sound in *vision, measure,* and *azure.* It is voiced from

the position used in producing the ʃ (which, as you remember, was unvoiced).

ɹ This inverted r has the value of the upright r, in words like *roar*, *aroused*, *derived*. This sound is voiced and is produced with the sides of the tongue anchored to the upper teeth ridge and the tip of the tongue free but pointing toward the hard palate.

ŋ This is the *ng* sound, as in *morning*, *evening*, and *singing*. It is voiced entirely through the nose, the back of the tongue being arched against the soft palate. It is not composed of the two separate sounds of *n* and *g* but is a single sound differing from both.

ɦ This is the voiced *h*, as in *behave*. Most of the time *h* will be unvoiced, as in *hot*, *heart*, *holy*, but when it appears between two vowels it is voiced. It is produced with the mouth open, tongue relaxed, using only the vocal cords.

ʍ This is the *hw* sound in *why*, *what*, *when*, *where*. It is made by blending two sounds in quick succession, a very short unvoiced *h* quickly followed by a longer, voiced *w*, formed by puckering the lips, the tongue all the while on the floor of the mouth.

tʃ This is the affricate in *chocolate*, *watch*, and *chimes*. Made up of the two sounds *t* and *ʃ*, said in quick succession, it is unvoiced.

dʒ This is the affricate ordinarily represented in English by the sound of the letter *j*, as in *judge*, *jaw*, *knowledge*. It is a voicing of the two successive sounds of *d* and *ʒ*, and it differs from tʃ only in being voiced.

So far we have eight new symbols representing ten sounds of American speech. Anyone who is mastering them for the first time will do well to halt here and make a set of ten flash cards, one for each sound, with the symbol on one side and one or more words containing the sound on the other side. Before continuing, flash the cards until you can articulate the appropriate sound for each symbol at a glance; be sure to whisper the unvoiced sounds (θ, ʃ, tʃ). This should take only a few minutes.

Now we are ready to go on to the other consonantal sounds, all of them with the familiar symbols of the regular alphabet.

p and b These are alike, except that one is unvoiced and the other is voiced, as in *peep* and *bob*. They are produced by placing the lips together for an instant and then exploding the sound between them.

m   This is hummed through the nose with the lips closed, as in *mum*.

w   This is produced as in *wail*, *win*, *wander* by voicing the sound through pursed lips.

d and *t*   These are alike, except that one is voiced and the other is unvoiced, as in *deed* and *tot*. The tip of the tongue touches the teeth ridge at the base of the upper teeth. The breath is stopped and then exploded as the tongue is relaxed.

n and *l*   These sounds are the same except that one is emitted through the nose, the other through the mouth, as in *none*, and *lull*. Notice the position of the tongue, the same as for *t* and *d*. *n* and *l* are *continuals*, that is, characterized by the continual, unstopped emission of tone, the *n* through the nose, the *l* laterally over the sides of the tongue and out the mouth.

s and *z*   As in *hiss* and *buzz*, these sounds are identical except that the first is unvoiced, the second voiced. The sides of the tongue should touch the ridge at the base of the upper teeth, with the tip free and pointing upward. The sound is produced by friction.

k and *g*   As in *cook* and *gag*, the first sound is unvoiced and the other is voiced, but they are formed identically with the back of the tongue arched against the soft palate. The breath is stopped and then exploded as the tongue is relaxed.

h   This is the unvoiced *h* as in *he*, *high*, *hollow*. With mouth open, tongue relaxed, the vocal cords only in use, it is a brief unvoiced breath.

j   Though this is a familiar symbol, you will need to learn a new sound for it—the sound of the traditional *y*, as in *yet*, *use*. It is voiced, the tip of the tongue gliding forward against the hard palate.

f and *v*   The first is unvoiced, the second voiced, as in *fluff*, *valve*. These sounds are produced by friction, the lower lip against the upper teeth.

We are now on our second plateau. It will be best to stop here and review the sixteen consonantal sounds we have just presented. Again, make a set of flash cards, a symbol to each card and a key word on the back of each; then rehearse the sound for each symbol, making sure to distinguish between voiced and unvoiced sounds. (The unvoiced sounds: *p*, *f*, *t*, *s*, *k*, *h*.) Practice until the distinction between voiced and unvoiced sounds is automatic. Then return to the ten new symbols which we gave you on the first plateau, and flash those cards two or three times. You have done enough for one day! When you return to pick up your work at the next level, run through the twenty-six flash cards which you have now prepared, making sure that you have them securely in mind. Then move on to the next level, which is the vowels:

While we will use the symbols *a*, *e*, *i*, *o*, and *u* in representing the fifteen vowels of spoken English, they will appear in such a new relationship that we may forget them for the time being. We shall learn these fifteen symbols in three groups, with a key sentence to remind us of each group:

Group I. Front vowels, made with relaxed lips, the tongue arched in front; the jaw dropping lower with each successive vowel.

"Lee will let fair Ann pass."

i	*Lee*	Also the sound in *machine, feet, meet*.
ɪ	*will*	Also the sound in *it, hit*, and *city*.
ɛ	*let*	The sound in *Evelyn, sent*, and *ever*.
e	*pale*	This is the sound with which the letter *a* is pronounced when the English alphabet is recited. As in *rate, late*.
æ	*Ann*	This is the flat *a* of *lack, happy, apple*.
a	*pass.*	Spoken mostly in the East, this sound is absent from most American speech. It is intermediate between the flat *a* (æ) and the broad *a* (a).

Group II. Back vowels, made with the lips rounded, the back of the tongue arched, the jaw dropping lower with each successive vowel:

"Who could obey all honest fathers?"

u	*Who*	Also the sound in *shoe, fool, tune*.
ʊ	*could*	Also the sound in *wood, good, put*.
o	*obey*	This sound is generally short and is to be distinguished from the long *o*, which is really a diphthong (see below).
ɔ	*all*	The same as in *awe, water, claw*.
ɒ	*honest*	This inverted *a* represents the sound in *hot, was, otter*.
ɑ	*fathers?*	This is the well-known broad *a*.

Group III. Middle vowels, made with the lips relaxed, the tongue arched in the middle.

"The bird won."

ə	*The*	This is the neutral vowel *uh*, short and unaccented, for weaker forms and for unaccented syllables. Above, after, open.

3   *bird*   W*ord, third, heard.* A vowel always followed by an *r*.

ʌ   *won.*   W*onder, sun, up.* Identical with the neutral vowel, except that it is long and usually accented.

Having reached the third plateau, let us now stop to consolidate our gains. Make flash cards for the fifteen vowels. Learn and repeat the three key sentences; then separate the vowel sounds from the key words and repeat each in a series as isolated sounds:

Group I: i, ɪ, ɛ, e, æ, ạ.
Group II: u, ʊ, o, ɔ, ᴅ, ɑ.
Group III: ə, ɜ, ʌ.

Continue flashing the cards and repeating the sentences and vowel groups until every symbol represents a clearly distinct sound. Very little remains to be done. In fact, you now know all the symbols, and it is only necessary to combine a few of the vowels to make the diphthongs:

In mastering the diphthongs, we shall use the method employed with the vowels, with a key sentence for each of three groups. A diphthong is formed by quickly gliding from one vowel to another, the first being the longer and the second short.

Group I. Diphthongs formed with the short ɪ sound:

"*Pay my boy.*"

ɛɪ   *Pay*   *Pray, say, day.* Made by combining the two sounds of *let* and *it*.

ɑɪ   *my*   *Sigh, high, light.* Made by combining the sounds of *far* and *it*.

ɔɪ   *boy.*   *Voice, noise, choice.* Made by combining the sounds of *awe* and *it*.

Group II. Dipthongs formed with the short ʊ sound:

"*Go now.*"

oʊ   *Go*   *Show, know, low.*

ɑʊ   *now.*   *How, south, mouth.* The initial vowel must be rounded, not flattened into æ.

Group III. Diphthongs formed with the neutral vowel ə. The second vowel in each of these four diphthongs is neutral. The initial vowels are in series, ɪ, ɛ, ʊ, ɔ:

"Here's their poor ore."

ɪə	*Here's*	*Earrings.*
ɛə	*their*	*wearing.*
ʊə	*poor*	*mooring.*
ɔʊ̆	*ore.*	*soaring.*

You have now reached the fourth and final plateau. Consolidate your gains by learning the three key sentences:

"Pay my boy. Go now. Here's their poor ore."

Alternate between repeating these sentences and the diphthongs contained within them, as with the vowels. Then go back and review all four plateaus. Review daily for at least a week.

The next step is to begin using your newly acquired phonetic alphabet in the recording of speech. The best way to do this is to single out individual words in the speeches you hear, words which seem to you to be mispronounced. Take the trouble to set them down in phonetic transcription. After you have done this for a time with the conversational talk around you and the public speeches of others, you are ready to apply the method to the recordings of your own speeches. The best reference guide for correct pronunciation is A *Pronouncing Dictionary of American English* by Kenyon and Knott (see Bibliography).

BIBLIOGRAPHY

BOOKS ON SERMON DELIVERY

Akin, Johnnye, Fessenden, Seth A., Larson, P. Merville, and Williams, Albert N. *Helping the Bible Speak.* Association Press, 1956. (Comprehensive and competent help from homiletics and speech specialists.)

Garrison, Webb B. *The Preacher and His Audience.* Revell, 1954. (One of the rare treatments of the preacher's relation to his congregation; many factors not presented in other current books.)

Jones, E. Winston. *Preaching and the Dramatic Arts.* Macmillan, 1948. (Largely a briefer presentation of the point of view of the Kirkpatrick book, below.)

Keighton, Robert E. *The Man Who Would Preach.* Abingdon, 1956. (The preacher himself as a part of his sermon.)

Kirkpatrick, Robert White. *The Creative Delivery of Sermons.* Macmillan, 1947. (Especially valuable for practical guidance in speaking in the emotional mode.)

Overstreet, H. A. *Influencing Human Behavior.* Norton, 1925.

Reed, David H. C. *The Communication of the Gospel.* SCM Press, 1952. (While broader than the topic of delivery, this book contains many helpful insights basic to good oral communication.)

Sleeth, Ronald E. *Persuasive Preaching.* Harper, 1956. (A teacher of homiletics writes with the benefit of technical speech training.)

ARTICULATION, VOICE, AND SPEECH

Anderson, Virgil A. *Training the Speaking Voice.* Oxford University Press, 1942. (A guide, employing the phonetic alphabet.)

Compere, Moiree (ed.). *Living Literature for Oral Interpretation.* Appleton-Century-Crofts, 1949.

Curry, Robert. *The Mechanism of the Human Voice.* Longmans, Green, 1940.

Curry, Samuel S. *Vocal and Literary Interpretation of the Bible.* Hodder and Stoughton, 1903. (The founder of the Boston School of Expression shows how his method may be used in reading the Bible aloud.)

Dixon, John. *How to Speak Here, There and On the Air.* Abingdon, 1949.

Eisenson, Jon. *The Psychology of Speech.* Crofts, 1939.

Fairbanks, Grant. *Voice and Articulation Drillbook.* Harper, 1940. (An abundance of practical helps, using the phonetic method.)

Fairbanks, Grant. *Practical Voice Practice*. Harper, 1944. (A book of useful drill materials for voice problems.)

Fields, U., and Bender, J. *Voice and Diction*. Macmillan, 1949.

Grace, William J., and Grace, J. C. *The Art of Communicating Ideas*. Devin-Adair, 1952.

Hahn, Elise, Lomas, Charles W., Hargis, Donald E., and Vandraegen, Daniel. *Basic Voice Training for Speech*. McGraw-Hill, 1952. (A comprehensive guide to speech improvement.)

Hoffman, William G. *Public Speaking Today*. McGraw-Hill, 1940.

Hoffman, William G. *How to Make Better Speeches*. Funk & Wagnalls, 1948.

Jacobson, Edmund. *Progressive Relaxation*. University of Chicago Press, 1929.

Jacobson, Edmund. *You Must Relax*. McGraw-Hill, 1934.

Judson, L., and Weaver, A. *Voice Science*. Crofts, 1942. (Detailed discussion of the speech mechanisms.)

Kenyon, John Samuel, and Knott, Thomas Albert. *A Pronouncing Dictionary of American English*. Merriam, 1949. (The standard phonetic dictionary of American speech.)

Lowry, Sara, and Johnson, Gertrude E. *Interpretative Reading, Techniques and Selections*. Appleton-Century-Crofts, 1942.

McCall, Roy C. *Fundamentals of Speech*. Macmillan, 1949.

McLean, Margaret Prendergast. *Good American Speech*. Dutton (rev. ed.), 1952. (An abundance of exercises, including a systematic guide to the phonetic method.)

Manser, R. *Speech Correction on the Contract Plan*. Prentice-Hall, 1951. (Systematic exercises for improving voice and articulation.

Mears, A. G. *The Right Way to Speak in Public*. Emerson, 1953.

Moses, Paul J. *The Voice of Neurosis*. Grune and Stratton, 1954. (An M.D. who has specialized in speech shows how voice may be used to interpret personality.)

Muehl, William. *The Road to Persuasion*. Oxford University Press, 1956. (The teacher of speech at Yale Divinity School has written a highly readable and exceedingly helpful book.)

Murray, E. *The Speech Personality*. Lippincott, 1944. (A comprehensive discussion of oral speech, language, and personality.)

Nemoy, E., and Davis, S. *The Correction of Defective Consonant Sounds*. Expression Co., 1945. (Detailed workbook providing suggestions and drill materials for correcting defective consonant sounds.)

Prochnow, Herbert V. *The Successful Speaker's Handbook*. Prentice-Hall, 1951.

Sarett, Lew, and Foster, W. T. *Basic Principles of Speech.* Houghton Mifflin, 1936. (A good text in general speech.)

Stanislavsky, Constantin. *An Actor Prepares.* Theatre Arts Inc., 1936. (The classic road to perceptual creativity, basic to melism.)

Van Riper, C. *Speech Therapy: A Book of Readings.* Prentice-Hall, 1953. (Abstracts of published articles relating to the major speech disorders.)

Van Riper, C. *Speech Correction Principles and Methods.* Prentice-Hall (rev. ed.), 1954. (General discussion involving causes and treatments of major speech disorders.)

West, R., Ansberry, M., and Carr, A. *The Rehabilitation of Speech.* Harper (rev. ed.), 1957. (General discussion of the major types of speech disorders of a clinical nature.)

SOME NOTED PREACHERS AND THEIR METHODS

Barstow, Lewis O. *Representative Modern Preachers.* Hodder and Stoughton, 1904.

Crocker, Lionel. *Henry Ward Beecher's Speaking Art.* Revell, 1937.

Currier, Albert H. *Nine Great Preachers.* Pilgrim Press, 1912.

Garvie, Alfred E. *The Preachers of the Church.* Doran, 1926.

Gray, Joseph M. M. *Prophets of the Soul.* Abingdon, 1936.

Horne, Charles Silvester. *The Romance of Preaching.* Revell, 1914. (Preaching as seen through great Christian preachers in history.)

Jones, Edgar DeWitt. *Lords of Speech.* Willett, Clark, 1937. Chap. IX, "Henry Ward Beecher"; Chap. XII, "Phillips Brooks."

Jones, Edgar DeWitt. *The Royalty of the Pulpit.* Harper, 1951. (A study of the persons who gave the Yale lectures on preaching.)

MacLeod, Donald (ed.). *Here Is My Method.* Revell, 1952. (Thirteen contemporary preachers tell how they prepare and deliver sermons.)

Newton, Joseph Fort. *Some Living Masters of the Pulpit.* Doran, 1923.

Prichard, Harold A. *The Minister, the Method, the Message.* Scribner's, 1932. Chap. V, "Preparation and Delivery." (A summary of the methods of many celebrated preachers.)

Storrs, Richard S. *Conditions of Success in Preaching Without Notes.* Dodd, Mead, 1875.

CHAPTERS AND ARTICLES ON SERMON DELIVERY

Baxter, Batsell Barrett. *The Heart of the Yale Lectures.* Macmillan, 1947. Chap. II, "Power of Personality"; Chap. VI, "Attitudes"; Chap. IX, "Delivery"; Chap. X, "Setting for the Sermon"; Part III, "The Congregation."

Beecher, Henry Ward. *Yale Lectures on Preaching* (First Series). J. B. Ford, 1872. Chap. VI, "Rhetorical Drill and General Training."

Blackwood, Andrew Watterson. *The Preparation of Sermons.* Abingdon, 1948. Chap. XVII, "The Preparation for Speaking"; Chap. XVIII, "The Delivery from the Pulpit"; Chap. XXIII, "The Sermon as an Act of Worship."

Booth, John Nicholls. *The Quest of Preaching Power.* Macmillan, 1943. Chap. X, "Handling Sermon Manuscripts Efficiently."

Broadus, John A. *On the Preparation and Delivery of Sermons.* New and revised edition by Jesse Burton Weatherspoon. Harper, 1944. Part IV, Chap. V, "Imagination in Preaching"; Part V, Chap. III, "Three Methods of Delivery"; Chap. IV, "On Delivery, As Regards Voice."

Brown, Charles Reynolds. *The Art of Preaching.* Macmillan, 1922. Chap. VI, "The Delivery of the Sermon."

Buttrick, Geo. A. *Jesus Came Preaching.* Scribner's, 1931. Chap. VI, "The Craftsmanship of the Preacher"; Chap. VII, "The Personality of the Preacher."

Cadman, S. Parkes. *Ambassadors of God.* Macmillan, 1920. Chap. VIII, "Preaching: Its Preparation and Practice"; Chap. IX, "Preaching and Worship."

Chappel, Clovis G. *Anointed to Preach.* Abingdon, 1951. Chap. V, "Our Finest Hour."

Cleland, James T. *The True and Lively Word.* Scribner's, 1954. Chap. IV, "The Word and the Words of the Preacher."

Farmer, Herbert H. *The Servant of the Word.* Nisbet, 1941. Chap. III, "Preaching as Personal Encounter."

Ferris, Theodore Parker. *Go Tell the People.* Scribner's, 1951. Chap. V, "Personal Problems of the Preacher."

Fuller, David Otis (ed.). *Spurgeon's Lectures to His Students.* Zondervan (2nd ed.), 1945. (Several chapters deal directly with sermon delivery.)

Garvie, Alfred E. *A Guide to Preachers.* Armstrong, 1906. Part III, Chap. I, "Personality in Preaching"; Chap. XIII, "The Delivery of a Sermon."

Garvie, Alfred E. *The Christian Preacher.* Scribner's, 1921. Part III, Chap. VI, "The Delivery of the Sermon."

Jeffrey, Geo. Johnstone. *This Grace Wherein We Stand.* Scribner's, 1949. Chap. IV, "The Ordeal Itself."

Jones, Ilion T. *Principles and Practice of Preaching.* Abingdon, 1956. Chap. 11, "Methods of Delivery"; Chap. 12, "Speech Mechanism."

Jordon, G. Ray. *You Can Preach!* Revell, 1951. Chap. 13, "Final

Preparation"; Chap. 16, "We Deliver the Sermon"; Chap. 18, "The Outline in the Pulpit."

Jowett, John H. *The Preacher, His Life and Work*. Doubleday, Doran, 1929. Chap. V, "The Preacher in His Pulpit."

Kennedy, Gerald. *His Word Through Preaching*. Harper, 1947. Part I, Chap. IV, "If the Trumpet Sound Indistinct."

Knox, John. *The Integrity of Preaching*. Abingdon, 1957. Chap. V, "Preaching Is Personal"; Chap. VI, "Preaching Is Worship."

Lantz, John Edward. *Speaking in the Church*. Macmillan, 1954. Chap. II, "Preparing and Using the Mind"; Chap. III, "Preparing and Using the Body"; Chap. IV, "Preparing and Using the Voice."

Lehman, H. T. *Heralds of the Gospel*. Muhlenberg, 1953. Chap. IV, "The Herald in His Pulpit."

Liske, Thomas V. *Effective Preaching*. Macmillan, 1951. Part I, "The Delivery of the Sermon."

Luccock, Halford E. *In the Minister's Workshop*. Abingdon, 1944. Chap. VIII, " 'Oft When the Word Is on Me to Deliver.' "

Luccock, Halford E. *Communicating the Gospel*. Harper, 1954. Chap. V, "The Preacher as a Craftsman."

Macartney, Clarence Edward. *Preaching Without Notes*. Abingdon, 1946. Chap. V, "Preaching Without Notes."

MacLennan, David A. *Pastoral Preaching*. Westminster, 1955. Chap. VI, "The Pastor Preaching."

Nes, William H. *The Excellency of the Word*. Morehouse-Gorham, 1956. Chap. II, "The Use of Images."

Oman, John. *Concerning the Ministry*. Harper, 1937. Chap. VII, "Personal Weight"; Chap. X, "Fervour and Its Substitutes"; Chap. XI, "Speaking."

Park, John Edgar. *The Miracle of Preaching*. Macmillan, 1936. Chap. VI, "Preaching, Delivery and Results."

Patton, Carl S. *The Preparation and Delivery of Sermons*. Willett, Clark, 1938. Chap. VII, "The Delivery of the Sermon."

Prior, Michael. "The Minister's Voice and Speech," *The Congregational Quarterly* (1957), 35:241-247.

Scherer, Paul. *For We Have This Treasure*. Harper, 1944. Chap. VI, "The Way You Handle the Word of Truth."

Sizoo, Joseph R. *Preaching Unashamed*. Abingdon, 1949. Chap. VII, "Words Are Not Enough."

Sockman, Ralph W. *The Highway of God*. Macmillan, 1942. Chap. II, "A Reed in the Wind"; Chap. III, "A Prophet"; Chap. IV, "More Than a Prophet."

Stidger, William L. *Preaching Out of the Overflow*. Cokesbury, 1929. (This book is helpful through its basic idea; several chapters bear directly on sermon delivery.)

INDEX

Monotony of rate, exercises to improve, 140
Morality, of ministers, misguided, 80-81; healthy, 81-82
Morrison, Charles Clayton, 108
Motor mindedness, 69

MacLaren, Alexander, 106
McLean, Margaret, 32

Nasality, 25-27; exercises to improve, 138-139, 147-148
Newton, Joseph Fort, 107
Norwood, Robert, 105
Notes, consulting of, 110; delivery without, 106-107; example of, 111-112; legibility of, 109-110; based on no manuscript, 105-107; use of: trial and error in, 109

Olfactory creativity, 151
Organic and functional speech disorders, 18
Overlaid function, speech as, 16-18

Pantomime, 60-61
Parish, minister in, 4
Pathos, 77-78
Pause, 36, 38-39, 85-86, 91
Personal counseling, 128-129; cost to counselee, 79; steps of, 79-80
Perceptual creativity; see Creativity
Personal power, 81
Personality, revealed by gesture, 71; revealed by posture, 71-72; sermon as index of, 1; and speech, 127-128; speech personality, 16; revealed by voice variables, 39
Pharisee, 80
Phrasing, 38-39
Phonation, 19
Phonetic alphabet, acquiring the, 32, 157-163
Phonetic transcription, 30

Pitch, 19-23; level and cultural norms, 20; optimum, 20
Posture, 71-72; exercises, 145
Practice, 48, 119
Preaching, as an art, 56
Preaching classes, importance of, 113-114; procedure, 114-119
Preparation versus delivery, 2
Pronunciation, 35

Radio and TV, 2
Range, 20-21
Rate, 35-37
Rating, emotions, 135; posture and gesture, 134; readings, 91-92; speeches, 12-13; voice variables, 133
Reading aloud, aids to, 86-88; like talking, 83-85; pausing, 85-86; troublesome words, 89-90
Reading, related to phrasing, 90
Redhead, John A., Jr., 104
Regionalisms, 26
Relaxation, 43-45; exercises, 144-145
Resonation, 24; exercises, 146-148
Resonators, flexibility of, 24
Rhythms, in speaking, 51-52
Robbins, Harold Chandler, 102
Robertson, F. W., 102

Script, preparing a, 90-91
Security, feelings of, 109
Self-instruction, 3-4, 10, 122-129
Seminary training, 3
Sensual imagery, 69
Sermons as seed, 57; doctrinal, 58
Short, John, 105
Sigmatism, 30; exercises to improve, 139
Smith, Dorothy, 32
Sockman, Ralph W., 104
Speaking ease, 5
Speech disorders, functional, 18; organic, 18
Speech mechanisms, 16-18